The Chicken SHACK

The *Chicken* SHACK

OVER 65 CLUCKIN' GOOD RECIPES THAT SHOWCASE THE BEST WAYS TO ENJOY CHICKEN

RYLAND PETERS & SMALL
LONDON • NEW YORK

Senior Designer Toni Kay
Desk Editor Emily Calder
Head of Production
 Patricia Harrington
Creative Director Leslie Harrington
Editorial Director Julia Charles

Indexer Hilary Bird

First published in 2022 by
Ryland Peters & Small
20–21 Jockey's Fields, London
WC1R 4BW and
341 E 116th St, New York NY 10029
www.rylandpeters.com

10 9 8 7 6 5 4 3 2 1

Recipe collection compiled by Emily
Calder. Text © Valerie-Aikman Smith,
Miranda Ballard, Ghillie Basan, Fiona
Beckett, Julz Beresford, Maxine Clark,
Ross Dobson, Ursula Ferrigno, Carol
Hilker, Jennifer Joyce, Jenny Linford,
Loretta Liu, Uyen Luu, Dan May,
Nitisha Patel, Louise Pickford, Laura
Santini, Milli Taylor, Jenny Tschiesche,
Sunil Vijayakar, Laura Washburn 2022.

Design & photography © Ryland
Peters & Small 2022 (see page 144
for picture credits).

ISBN: 978-1-78879-442-8

A CIP record for this book is available
from the British Library.
US Library of Congress Cataloging-in-
Publication Data has been applied for.

Printed and bound in China.

Notes:
• Both British (Metric) and
American (Imperial plus US cups)
measurements are included in
these recipes for your convenience,
however it is important to work with
one set of measurements and not
alternate between the two within
a recipe.
• All spoon measurements are
level unless otherwise specified.
• Uncooked eggs should not be
served to the very old, frail, young
children, pregnant women or those
with compromised immune systems.
• Ovens should be preheated
to the specified temperatures.
We recommend using an oven
thermometer. If using a fan-assisted
oven, adjust temperatures according
to the manufacturer's instructions.
• When a recipe calls for the grated
zest of citrus fruit, buy unwaxed fruit
and wash well before using. If you
can only find treated fruit, scrub well
in warm soapy water before using.
• To sterilize screw-top jars and
bottles for storing dressings, preheat
the oven to 150°C fan/160°C/325°F/
Gas 3. Wash the jars and/or bottles
and their lids in hot soapy water then
rinse but don't dry them. Remove any
rubber seals, put the jars onto
a baking sheet and into the oven for
10 minutes. Soak the lids in boiling
water for a few minutes.
• Before serving poultry, make sure
it is steaming hot and cooked all the
way through. When you cut into the
thickest part of the meat, check that
none of the meat is pink and that any
juices run clear. In a whole bird this
is the area between the leg and the
breast. Ensure all tools and working
surfaces are cleaned, and hands are
washed, before and after handling
raw meat.

Contents

Introduction

A classic staple, chicken is a tasty, protein-rich and delicious base for anyone who enjoys the convenience and satisfaction of including poultry in their diet. Chicken is not only a food that is easy to come by, but it is also hugely versatile. Not only does it pair beautifully with carbohydrates (Fried chicken sandwich, anyone?), but it is delicious and filling for those keen include more protein as part of a healthy, balanced diet. Whether accompanied by a silky pasta dish or a Vietnamese salad, it cannot be denied that chicken is at the heart of so many of our most-loved meals.

Chicken is quite famously not only a nutritious treat, but for many it is a food symbolic of family, friends and good times. Many of us perhaps associate chicken with delicious smells wafting from family kitchens on a Sunday afternoon before we tuck into succulent slices of chicken nestled in-between crispy roast potatoes, fresh vegetables and golden Yorkshire puddings. Or maybe chicken reminds us of exciting afternoons of sport (over 1 million chicken wings were consumed over the course of the Super Bowl in 2012), and late nights spent joking around with friends over a portion of crunchy chicken tenders and fries. There are endless ways to make memories with chicken – whether this be a creamy Chicken Tikka Masala paired with basmati rice and pillowy naan bread, a Chicken Panini with melty Gouda and caramelised red onions, or a Mustard & Herb Chicken baked in a salt crust.

The Chicken Shack provides more than 65 delicious and exciting recipes for everything from succulent nibbles to spicy curries and comforting sandwiches. Some are the classic and simple uses of chicken, stuffing and roasting the bird with generous flavours and seasonings, whilst some offer more inventive dishes for hosting or for jazzing up a mid-week dinner. Those who love to host will relish the 'Tasty Titbits' such as Crispy Garlic Chive Chicken Wontons, Spicy Chicken Kebabs with ground almonds and Chicken & Potato Cream Stew Dumplings. Anyone seeking an indulgent treat – think melting cheese, or licking leftover wing sauce from your fingers – can look to Extra-Crunchy Crumbed Wings, Buffalo Bingo Wings with homemade ranch dressing, or Barbecue Chicken & Two Cheeses Mac 'n' Cheese. For everything from working from home lunches to Friday night bites, 'Fun in a Bun' provides inspiration for bites such as a Tandoori Chicken Grilled Cheese with paneer & mango chutney, Shredded Chicken Tacos and Chicken Caesar Sliders wrapped in Parma ham with Caesar dressing. If you're looking to spice up your life a little, the 'Spicy & Saucy' chapter offers Indian Pepper Chicken, Chicken Fajitas and Butter Chicken. Finally, for traditional and impressive uses of chicken, look no further than 'Chic Chicken', featuring Chicken with 40 cloves of garlic, Crispy Gravy Chicken Spaghetti and Chicken Pot Pie. Get ready to bring all of these dishes and more into the comfort of your home!

Tasty Titbits

Spicy chicken & prawn dumplings

A simple and delicious favourite served with a garlic, ginger and chilli/chile oil.

For the wheat dough

150 g/1 cup + 2 tablespoons
  Asian white wheat flour
80 ml/scant ⅓ cup water

For the filling

1 skinless, boneless chicken breast
60 g/2¼ oz. raw prawns/shrimp,
  peeled and deveined
1 leek, chopped
2 Chinese chive stalks, chopped
a large handful of fresh coriander/
  cilantro, coarsely chopped
½ –1 tablespoon Korean hot pepper powder
  (to taste)
1 teaspoon freshly ground black pepper
1 tablespoon oyster sauce
½ tablespoon sesame oil

For the dipping sauce

1 garlic clove, crushed
1 tablespoon freshly grated ginger
6 tablespoons soy sauce
2 tablespoons chilli/chile oil

MAKES 16

First, prepare the wheat dough. Place the flour in a large mixing bowl and combine with the water to form a dough. Turn the dough out onto a lightly floured surface and knead for 20–25 minutes or until the dough is smooth and elastic. Separate and roll into 2 equal cylinders about 2.5 cm/1 inch in diameter. Cover with a damp tea towel/kitchen cloth and set aside to rest for 30 minutes.

Meanwhile, mince the chicken breast and prawns using a sharp knife to chop. Transfer to a mixing bowl and combine with the rest of the filling ingredients. Chill in the fridge for 30 minutes.

To prepare the skins, use a sharp knife to slice each dough cylinder into 8 equal pieces. On a lightly floured surface, flatten each piece with a rolling pin until it has a round shape and a diameter of around 7.5 cm/3 inches.

Put a large teaspoon of filling into the centre of each skin. Dip your fingertips in a small dish of water and slightly moisten the edge of half the skin. Seal the dumpling tightly using your fingers to pinch, pull and fold the skin into 4 or 5 pleats at the join. Repeat the process until all the mixture and skins have been used. Bring a large pan of water to boiling point. Gently lower in the dumplings and cover with a lid to poach. The dumplings are cooked when they float to the top of the water.

To make the dipping sauce, mix together all the ingredients. Drain the dumplings and serve at once accompanied with the dipping sauce.

Note If you prefer a crispy base, you can lightly pan-fry the uncooked dumplings in a small amount of oil and to finish off the cooking process, place the dumplings in a large pan of boiling water. Cover with a lid and poach until they float to the surface.

Chicken & potato cream stew dumplings

These dumplings are a delicious bite-sized treat, especially when they are dipped into the hot melted butter.

For the crystal skin dough
100 g/³⁄₄ cup wheat starch
50 g/½ cup tapioca starch
a pinch of fine sea salt
150 ml/²⁄₃ cup boiling (not hot) water

For the filling
2 tablespoons unsalted butter
½ onion, finely diced
½ carrot, finely diced
½ celery stalk, finely diced
1 potato, peeled and finely diced
1 tablespoon plain/all-purpose flour
1 chicken stock cube
175 ml/³⁄₄ cup milk
1 skinless, boneless chicken breast, finely diced
½ teaspoon sea salt
½ teaspoon freshly ground black pepper
melted butter, for dipping

a bamboo steamer, lined with parchment paper

MAKES 16

First, prepare the crystal skin dough. In a large mixing bowl, combine the wheat starch, tapioca starch and salt. Add the boiling water and mix with a wooden spoon until a dough is formed. Transfer to a lightly floured surface and knead until smooth. Separate the dough in half and roll into 2 equal cylinders, about 2.5 cm/1 inch in diameter. Wrap in clingfilm/plastic wrap and rest until needed.

Melt the butter in a large pan over a medium heat. Add the diced onion, carrot, celery and potato. Cook, stirring occasionally, until tender, about 3–4 minutes.

Whisk in the flour slowly and heat for a minute. Next, crumble the stock cube into the pan and gradually add the milk, whisking constantly. Continue cooking and stirring until the sauce has slightly thickened, about 1–2 minutes.

Add the chicken. Bring the sauce to a boil; reduce the heat and simmer until the potatoes and chicken are tender, about 12–15 minutes. Set aside to cool.

While the filling is cooling, divide the dough into 16 equal balls. On a lightly floured surface use a rolling pin to flatten the dough balls into thin discs, about 5 cm/2 inches in diameter. Cover the finished skins with a damp tea towel/kitchen cloth as you work so that they don't dry out. Place a large teaspoon of filling into the centre of each skin. Fold the dumplings in half and pinch the edges together to form a simple crescent shape.

Space out the dumplings evenly in the bamboo steamer lined with parchment paper. Steam over boiling water for 15–20 minutes or until the skins turn transparent. Serve warm with the hot melted butter for dipping.

Red curry chicken & lentil bao

A taste of Thailand fused with traditional Chinese bao (or baozi to give them their full name) in these beautiful red curry buns.

For the bread dough

2 teaspoons dry easy-bake/
    fast-action yeast
450 g/3½ cups Asian white
    wheat flour
100 g/¾ cup plus 1 tablespoon
    icing/confectioners' sugar, sifted
15 g/2 tablespoons dried milk powder
¼ teaspoon fine sea salt
2 teaspoons baking powder
180 ml/¾ cup water, add more
    if needed
50 ml/scant ¼ cup vegetable oil,
    plus extra for oiling the bowl

For the filling

1 tablespoon sunflower oil
2 onions, finely chopped
2 garlic cloves, crushed
1–2 tablespoons Thai red curry paste
    (to taste)
2 skinless, boneless chicken breasts,
    cut into bite-sized pieces
500 ml/2 cups hot chicken stock
80 g/scant ½ cup dried red lentils

a bamboo steamer, lined with
    parchment paper

MAKES 16

Place the yeast in a large mixing bowl, then add the flour, sugar, milk powder, salt and baking powder. Make sure the yeast is separated from the salt by the layer of flour. Add the water and oil and bring together with a dough scraper. When no dry flour remains, remove the dough from the bowl and place on a lightly floured surface. Knead firmly for 5–10 minutes. Lightly oil the mixing bowl. Shape the dough into 2 cylinders and place back in the oiled bowl, cover with oiled clingfilm/plastic wrap and leave in a warm place to rise for 40–60 minutes or until doubled in size.

While the dough is rising, prepare the filling. Heat the oil in a large frying pan/skillet and add the onions. Cook for 3 minutes over a gentle heat. Stir in the crushed garlic and curry paste and cook for 1–2 minutes more. Add the chicken pieces and cook for 2–3 minutes. Stir in the stock and lentils, bring to a boil, cover and simmer for 25 minutes, stirring occasionally, until the lentils are tender and the chicken is cooked. Set aside to cool.

Remove the risen dough from the bowl, punch it down and knead it again briefly, but very carefully rather than firmly. Roll the dough out into a big rectangle and portion it out into 16 equal balls. Cover the dough balls with oiled clingfilm/plastic wrap and leave to rest again for 30 minutes in a warm place.

Roll out each ball to a diameter of around 7.5 cm/3 inches trying to make the centre slightly thicker than the edges to hold the filling. Cover each dough circle with a damp tea towel/kitchen cloth.

Once the skins are ready, place 1 tablespoon of the filling in the centre of each round. Gather and pleat the edges, pinching to seal the top of the bun. Set the finished buns in the lined bamboo steamer about 5 cm/2 inches apart. You may have to do this in batches depending on the size of your steamer. Cover with oiled clingfilm/plastic wrap and allow to rise for another 30 minutes. Once risen, steam the bao over a high heat for 15–20 minutes or until the dough is light and fluffy. Cool slightly and serve.

Crispy garlic chive chicken wontons

Deep-frying these dumplings until they are crisp transforms them into an appetizing snack. When served with the dipping sauce, they go perfectly with pre-dinner drinks. Chinese black rice vinegar is available from Asian stores.

1 skinless, boneless chicken breast fillet, finely diced

4 tablespoons fresh Chinese chives, finely chopped

a pinch of ground Sichuan pepper

1 teaspoon light soy sauce

½ teaspoon sesame oil

16 wonton wrappers

sunflower or vegetable oil, for deep frying

sea salt and freshly ground black pepper

For the dipping sauce

2 tablespoons Chinese black rice vinegar

1 teaspoon sugar

1 garlic clove, crushed

½ red chilli/chile, deseeded and finely chopped (optional)

SERVES 4

Mix together the ingredients for the dipping sauce and set aside. Thoroughly mix together the diced chicken, Chinese chives, Sichuan pepper, soy sauce and sesame oil. Season well with salt and pepper.

Take a wonton wrapper and place a teaspoon of the chicken mixture in the centre of the wrapper. Brush the edges with a little cold water and bring the wrapper together over the chicken to form a parcel, pressing together well to seal properly. Set aside. Repeat the process until all 16 wrappers have been filled.

Heat the oil in a large saucepan until very hot. Add 4 of the wontons and fry for a few minutes, until golden brown on both sides, turning over halfway through to ensure even browning. Remove with a slotted spoon and drain on paper towels/kitchen paper. Now repeat the process with the remaining wontons.

Serve at once with the dipping sauce.

Moroccan chicken puffs

These tasty nibbles encompass flavoursome notes of Moroccan cuisine, and are perfect to serve at social gatherings.

500 g/1 lb. 2 oz. store-bought
    puff pastry
1 egg, beaten
sesame seeds, for sprinkling

For the chicken mix

2 tablespoons olive oil
1 onion, finely chopped
3 garlic cloves, crushed
½ teaspoon ground ginger
¼ teaspoon ground cinnamon
a small pinch of saffron
¼ teaspoon ground cumin
1 small preserved lemon, chopped,
    seeds and pith removed
4 chicken thighs, boned,
    skinned and diced
¼ teaspoon smoked paprika
freshly ground black pepper
1 tablespoon freshly chopped
    flat-leaf parsley
1 tablespoon freshly chopped
    coriander/cilantro

7.5-cm/3-inch pastry/cookie cutter
a baking sheet, lined with
    parchment paper

MAKES 30–35

Preheat the oven to 180°C (350°F) Gas 4.

For the chicken mix, heat the oil in a frying pan/skillet and sauté the onion and garlic for 5 minutes. Add all of the other chicken mix ingredients to the pan, except the seasoning and herbs. Fry until the chicken is cooked through and the onion and garlic softened.

When the chicken is cooked, cool for a few minutes before seasoning with black pepper and adding the fresh herbs. Once completely cooled, roll out the puff pastry until 3 mm/⅛ inch thick and use the pastry/cookie cutter to cut it into rounds.

Place 1 teaspoonful of the chicken mix in the middle of each disk and then pinch the edges together, like a dumpling. Place the puffs pinch-side down on the prepared baking sheet 2.5 cm/1 inch apart and brush the tops with the beaten egg. Sprinkle with sesame seeds and bake in the preheated oven for 15–20 minutes until golden. Serve at once.

Chicken with garlic bites

A classic that can be found in any good tapas restaurant, these garlicky titbits are sure to hit the spot every time.

1 tablespoon paprika

1 tablespoon plain/all-purpose flour

1.75 kg/3¾ lb. skinless, boneless chicken pieces, such as thighs and breasts (no drumsticks)

100 ml/⅓ cup plus 1 tablespoon extra virgin olive oil

15 garlic cloves, bruised

1 fresh bay leaf

125 ml/½ cup plus 1 teaspoon medium dry sherry

1 tablespoon freshly chopped flat-leaf parsley, plus extra to serve

sea salt and freshly ground black pepper

a heat-diffusing mat

SERVES 4

Put the paprika, flour, salt and pepper in a plastic bag and shake to mix. Add the chicken pieces and toss again until the chicken is evenly coated. Leave in the bag for 30 minutes or longer.

Heat the olive oil in a frying pan/skillet, add the garlic and fry for 2 minutes, then remove with a slotted spoon. Add the chicken pieces (if necessary do half at a time, but remember to remove half the garlic-infused oil) and fry for 5 minutes. Add the fried garlic and continue frying for 5 more minutes until the chicken is golden.

Add the bay leaf and sherry and bring to a boil. Lower the heat and simmer gently on a heat-diffusing mat for about 30 minutes until tender. (Breast pieces will cook faster, so remove them about 10 minutes before the end of cooking.) Pile onto a serving platter and sprinkle with parsley.

Note Although this dish is traditionally cooked on top of the stove, it could be baked in a preheated oven at 190°C (375°F) Gas 5 for 35 minutes or until cooked through.

Sriracha & lime grilled chicken wings

You can also use regular lime juice and leaves in this dish to add a pleasant, cooling contrast to all the spices. Chicken wings are a fun appetizer to hand around or to take on a picnic.

24 chicken wings, halved at the joints, tips removed
60 m/¼ cup sriracha
60ml/¼ cup sambal oelek
180 ml/¾ cup dark runny honey
125 ml/½ cup toasted sesame oil
4 garlic cloves
2 mukrat limes, or regular limes, quartered
6 mukrat lime leaves, or regular lime leaves, shredded
1 onion, roughly chopped
sea salt and freshly ground black pepper,
1 tablespoon black sesame seeds
vegetable oil, for brushing the grate

To serve
tangerine wedges

SERVES 4–6

Place the chicken wings in a large ceramic dish or bowl. Then place the sriracha, sambal oelek, honey, sesame oil, garlic, lime quarters, lime leaves and onion in a blender and process until you have a smooth sauce. Season with salt and pepper. Pour the sauce over the chicken wings and toss to coat. Cover and refrigerate for at least 4 hours, or overnight if you have time.

When you are ready to cook, remove the chicken wings from the fridge and bring to room temperature. Heat the grill/barbecue to medium-high. Brush the grate with oil. Cook the wings on the grill for 6–8 minutes, then turn them over and either turn the heat down or move to a cooler part of the grill. Continue to cook for a further 8 minutes, turning occasionally to make sure they are cooked through and crispy on the outside.

Place the cooked wings on a large plate and sprinkle with the sesame seeds. Serve with the tangerine wedges.

Chicken shish kebabs with garlic sauce

Like most Middle-Eastern foods, these kebabs/kabobs are perfect for sharing. The garlic sauce is simple to make using easy-to-source ingredients and will keep refrigerated in an airtight container for several days.

For the garlic sauce

12 garlic cloves, crushed
125 ml/½ cup plus 1 teaspoon mayonnaise
1 teaspoon sea salt
125 ml/½ cup plus 1 teaspoon olive oil
1 tablespoon lemon juice, freshly squeezed

For the kebabs

125 ml/½ cup plus 1 teaspoon extra virgin olive oil
4 garlic cloves, crushed
65 ml/¼ cup plus 1 teaspoon lemon juice, freshly squeezed
2½ tablespoons freshly chopped flat-leaf parsley
1 kg/2 lb. 4 oz. chicken thigh fillets, trimmed and cubed
sea salt and freshly ground black pepper

To serve

4 handfuls of soft green salad leaves
2 tomatoes, cut into wedges
1 cucumber, peeled and sliced
8 soft wheat flour tortillas
lemon wedges, for squeezing

10–12 wooden skewers, soaked in cold water

SERVES 4

To make the garlic sauce, put the garlic and salt in a small food processor and process until finely chopped. Add the mayonnaise. With the motor still running, add the olive oil in a very slow trickle, until all of the oil has been incorporated and the sauce is smooth. Stir in the lemon juice and season to taste with black pepper. Set aside.

Put the olive oil, garlic, lemon juice, parsley and 1 teaspoon salt in a large, non-reactive bowl and whisk with a fork. Add the chicken and use your hands to toss until evenly coated. Season well and cover with clingfilm/plastic wrap. Let sit at cool room temperature for 1 hour.

Preheat the grill/broiler to medium/high. Thread the chicken onto the prepared skewers. Cook the kebabs for 4–5 minutes, turning occasionally, until the chicken is golden and cooked through.

Arrange the salad leaves, tomatoes and cucumber on serving plates. Put the kebabs on top and drizzle with the sauce. Serve with warmed tortillas and lemon wedges for squeezing.

Spicy chicken kebabs
with ground almonds

The combination of ground almonds and browned onions in the marinade gives these kebabs/kabobs a sweet, rich flavour.

700 g/1 lb. 9 oz skinless, boneless chicken breasts, cut into bite-sized pieces
juice of 1 lemon, freshly squeezed
1 teaspoon sea salt
1–2 tablespoons peanut or sunflower oil
1 onion, halved and sliced
2–3 tablespoons freshly grated ginger
2 garlic cloves, crushed
2–3 tablespoons ground almonds
1–2 teaspoons garam masala
125 ml/½ cup plus 1 tablespoon thick double/heavy cream

To serve
1–2 tablespoons butter
2–3 tablespoons blanched, flaked/slivered almonds
a small bunch of fresh flat-leaf parsley, finely chopped
warmed flatbreads

4 long, thin metal skewers

SERVES 4

First toss the chicken pieces in the lemon juice and salt to blanch them. Put aside for 15 minutes.

Meanwhile, heat the oil in a frying pan/skillet. Add the onion and cook until golden brown and crisp. Remove the onion from the oil and spread it out on a sheet of kitchen paper towels/kitchen paper to drain and cool. Reserve the oil in the frying pan/skillet.

Using a mortar and pestle, or an electric blender, pound the onions to a paste and beat in the ginger and garlic. Add the almonds and garam masala and bind with the cream. Tip the almond and onion mixture over the chicken and mix well. Cover and leave in the fridge to marinate for about 6 hours.

Thread the chicken onto the skewers and brush them with the reserved onion oil. Prepare a charcoal or conventional grill/broiler. Cook the kebabs for 3–4 minutes on each side, until the chicken is nicely browned and cooked through. Quickly melt the butter in a frying pan/skillet and stir in the flaked almonds until golden. Toss in the parsley and spoon the mixture over the grilled/broiled chicken. Serve hot with warmed flatbreads, if liked.

Lemon chicken kebabs
wrapped in aubergine

This Ottoman kebab/kabob dish is impressive and tasty and best served with a refreshing salad, such as tomato and cucumber, or parsley, (bell) pepper and onion, and rice.

juice of 2–3 lemons, freshly squeezed
2 garlic cloves, crushed
4–6 allspice berries, crushed
1 tablespoon crushed dried sage leaves
8 skinless, boneless chicken thighs
4 aubergines/eggplants
sea salt
sunflower oil, for deep-frying
1 tablespoon butter

To serve
lemon wedges, for squeezing
your choice of salad
your choice of rice

4 metal or wooden skewers (optional)
an ovenproof dish, well-greased

SERVES 4

In a shallow bowl, mix together the lemon juice, garlic, allspice berries and sage leaves. Toss the chicken thighs in the mixture, rolling them over in the juice, and let marinate for about 2 hours.

Preheat the oven to 180°C (350°F) Gas 4.

Peel the aubergines in strips and slice them thinly lengthways, so that you have at least 16 long strips. Soak the strips in a bowl of cold, salted water for about 30 minutes. Drain them and squeeze out the excess water. In a wok or frying pan/skillet, heat sufficient oil for deep-frying and fry the aubergines in batches, until golden brown. Drain on paper towels/kitchen paper.

On a board or plate, lay 2 aubergine strips, one over the other in a cross, then place a marinated chicken thigh in the middle. Pull the aubergine strips over the thigh to form a neat parcel. Place the aubergine parcel, seam-side down, in the prepared ovenproof dish and repeat the process with the remaining thighs. Pour the rest of the marinade over the top and dab each parcel with butter. Cover the dish with foil and cook in the preheated oven for 30 minutes. Remove the foil, baste the chicken parcels with the cooking juices, and return to the oven for a further 10 minutes. Serve immediately, threaded onto skewers to secure them (if using), with wedges of lemon on the side for squeezing and a salad and rice.

Dirty & Delicious

For the holy trinity paste

200 g/7 oz. green chillies/chiles, deseeded
200 g/7 oz. garlic cloves
200 g/7 oz. fresh root ginger
50 ml/3½ tablespoons vegetable oil
1 tablespoon sea salt

For the wings

2 tablespoons vegetable oil
1 teaspoon sea salt
3 teaspoons Holy Trinity Paste
juice of 1 lemon, freshly squeezed
1 teaspoon ground cumin
1 teaspoon ground coriander
1 teaspoon ground turmeric
1 teaspoon paprika
½ teaspoon dried chilli/ hot red pepper flakes
½ teaspoon tandoori masala
2 tablespoons natural/plain yogurt
1 teaspoon red chilli/chili powder
1 teaspoon dried fenugreek leaves
1 kg/2¼ lb. chicken wings, halved at the joints, tips removed

To serve

your choice of dipping sauce or chutney
lime wedges, for squeezing

a large baking sheet
a griddle pan (or heavy-based frying pan/skillet)

SERVES 4

Smokin' fiery chicken wings

Wings are a favourite – they are moist, tender and oh, so flavoursome! This recipe uses 'Holy Trinity Paste', which is used in a lot of the recipes in this book. These instructions make 625 g/2½ cups, and it can be kept in the fridge for up to 2 weeks.

First, make the Holy Trinity Paste. Blitz together the ingredients in a food processor to form a coarse paste. This can be kept in the fridge for up to 2 weeks.

In a large mixing bowl, combine all of the ingredients apart from the chicken wings. Mix well until the mixture is smooth, then add in the chicken wings and mix to coat. Allow the wings to marinate overnight in the fridge, if possible, or for a minimum of 30 minutes at room temperature.

Preheat the oven to 180°C (350°F) Gas 4.

Heat a griddle pan until smoking (if you don't have a griddle pan you can use a heavy-based frying pan/skillet). Seal the wings in the hot pan to create a smoky, charred flavour on the skin. Transfer the wings to a large baking sheet and bake in the preheated oven for 25 minutes.

Serve as a snack or appetizer with a dipping sauce or chutney and a squeeze of lime for a final flourish of zestiness.

Cornflake chicken nuggets *with sweet potato fries & roasted cherry tomatoes*

These nuggets are absolutely delicious, and have a slightly more healthy and exciting feel than a traditional breadcrumb coating. The sweet potato fries and roasted cherry tomatoes really lift the flavours, and add a gorgeous colour to the plate.

2 sweet potatoes, peeled and sliced into
  1-cm/½-inch thick fries
1 teaspoon olive oil
¾ teaspoon sea salt
120 g/5 cups cornflakes
1 egg
125 ml/½ cup milk
1 tablespoon arrowroot powder
¼ teaspoon garlic salt
4 skinless, boneless chicken breasts, chopped
  into 4 x 2-cm/1½ x ¾-inch nuggets
16 cherry tomatoes on the vine

2 large baking sheets

SERVES 4

Preheat the oven to 200°C (400°F) Gas 6.

Put the sweet potatoes on a baking sheet, drizzle over the olive oil and sprinkle over ½ teaspoon salt. Bake in the preheated oven for 35 minutes.

Meanwhile, grind the cornflakes in a food processor to fine crumbs. Alternatively, put the cornflakes in a freezer bag, close the bag tightly and bash the cornflakes with a rolling pin. Place in a bowl. In another small bowl, whisk the egg, add the milk, arrowroot, garlic salt and ¼ teaspoon salt.

Dip the chicken nuggets into the egg mixture, then into the cornflakes to cover and put onto a separate baking sheet. Put the chicken nuggets in the oven with the sweet potatoes for the last 10 minutes of baking. Add the tomatoes to the sweet potatoes for the last 10 minutes. Serve immediately.

Honey-fried chicken

Fried chicken is one of the world's most popular foods and each culture has their own version. Some like buttermilk-fried chicken, some prefer extra-crispy, double fried chicken and others, particularly in the American south with a sweet tooth, prefer this delicious honey-fried version.

1.8-kg/4-lb. chicken, cut into pieces
170 g/½ cup runny honey
1 tablespoon garlic powder
1 packet chicken bouillon granules
260 g/2 cups plain/all-purpose flour
1 litre/quart vegetable oil, for frying
sea salt and freshly ground black pepper

To serve
creamed corn, or your choice of other
    vegetable side (optional)

SERVES 4

Season the chicken pieces with salt and pepper, then coat each seasoned piece with honey.

In a shallow dish or bowl, mix together the garlic powder, chicken bouillon granules and flour. Dredge the honey-coated chicken pieces in the flour mixture, coating completely.

Fill a large, heavy-based frying-pan/skillet with oil to a depth of 2.5 cm/1 inch and heat over a medium-high heat until the oil is bubbling steadily.

In batches, fry the chicken for at least 8 minutes per side, until it's no longer pink and until the juices run clear. Make sure you reheat the oil so it's bubbling steadily before frying the next batch.

Serve with creamed corn or other vegetables (if desired).

Extra-crunchy crumbed wings

These wings are the perfect combination of textures – tender, soft meat enclosed in a crisp, herbed coating.

1.8 kg/4 lb. chicken wings, halved at the joints, tips removed
500 ml/2 cups buttermilk (optional)
4 eggs, beaten
100 g/¾ cup sesame seeds
100 g/¾ cup plain/all-purpose flour
1 tablespoon sea salt
½ teaspoon cayenne pepper
250 g/4 cups fresh breadcrumbs
4 garlic cloves, crushed

For the soy-caramel dipping sauce

75 g/⅓ cup caster/white granulated sugar
4–5 large shallots, chopped
1 garlic clove, crushed
½ tablespoon freshly grated ginger
3 tablespoons soy sauce
3 tablespoons rice vinegar (not seasoned)
335 ml/1⅓ cups water
2 tablespoons cornflour/cornstarch
1 tablespoon lemon juice, freshly squeezed (optional)

2–3 baking sheets, lined with parchment paper

SERVES 4–6

If using buttermilk, put the wings and buttermilk in a medium bowl and cover. Refrigerate overnight, or for at least 4 hours.

Preheat the oven to 190°C (375°F) Gas 5.

Remove the wings from the buttermilk and discard the milk. Place the wings in a large bowl, add the eggs and toss to coat.

Combine the sesame seeds, flour, salt, cayenne pepper, breadcrumbs and garlic in a small bowl. Dip each wing into the sesame mixture to fully coat. Place the coated wings side by side on the prepared baking sheets.

Bake in the preheated oven for 30 minutes, then increase the oven temperature to 200°C (400°F) Gas 6. Cook for a further 20–30 minutes, until the wings are golden brown and sizzling, and the juices run clear when the thickest part is pierced to the bone.

Whilst the wings are in the oven, make the dipping sauce. Start by cooking the sugar in a large, dry, heavy-based saucepan over a medium-high heat, undisturbed, until it melts around edges and begins to turn a perfect golden colour.

Add the shallots (use caution as the caramel will bubble up and steam vigorously) and cook for about 45 seconds, stirring, until the shallots shrink and become fragrant. Add the garlic and ginger and cook, stirring, for 30 seconds. Stir in the soy sauce, vinegar and water and simmer for 1 minute, stirring, until any hardened caramel has dissolved. The sauce will become a rich auburn colour.

Mix the cornflour with 2 tablespoons water until smooth, then stir into the sauce and simmer for 2 minutes, stirring occasionally. Remove from the heat and plunge the pan into a sink of cold water to stop the caramel cooking. If using lemon juice, stir it in now. Cover the sauce and keep warm. Remove the wings from the baking sheets and serve with the dipping sauce.

Buttermilk-crumbed wings

The best fried chicken always involves buttermilk, with the tangy marinade making it one of the juiciest and tastiest ways to cook chicken. This recipe is a classic.

For the dijon-blue cheese dipping sauce

100 ml/½ cup mayonnaise
120 ml/½ cup sour cream
2 teaspoons lemon juice, freshly squeezed
2 teaspoons red wine vinegar
1 teaspoon creamy Dijon mustard
¼ teaspoon Worcestershire sauce
50 g/⅓ cup crumbled blue cheese
1 garlic clove, crushed
1–2 tablespoons freshly chopped
    flat-leaf parsley
1 spring onion/scallion, finely chopped
sea salt and freshly ground black pepper

For the wings

3 eggs
500 ml/2 cups buttermilk
1.8 kg/4 lb. chicken wings, halved
    at the joints, tips removed
400 g/3 cups plain/all-purpose flour
60 g/1 cup crushed saltine crackers
    or cornflakes
1 teaspoon freshly ground black pepper
1 teaspoon dried thyme
¼ teaspoon cayenne pepper
1 teaspoon sea salt, plus extra to season
½ teaspoon garlic powder
vegetable oil, for frying

2–3 baking sheets, lined with foil
a deep fryer

SERVES 4

First, prepare the dipping sauce. Stir or whisk the mayonnaise, sour cream, lemon juice, vinegar, mustard and Worcestershire sauce in a bowl until smooth. Add the blue cheese, garlic, parsley and spring onion, and stir until combined. Season to taste, then cover and refrigerate for at least 1 hour before serving.

Beat the eggs and buttermilk together in a large bowl until smooth. Mix in the chicken wings, cover, and refrigerate for 30 minutes.

Preheat the oven to 220°C (425°F) Gas 7.

Combine the flour and crackers with the pepper, thyme, cayenne pepper, salt and garlic powder in a large bowl. Remove the chicken wings from the buttermilk marinade and discard the remaining marinade.

Allow the excess buttermilk to drip from the wings, then press into the crumbs to coat. Arrange the chicken wings on the prepared baking sheets. Bake in the preheated oven for 25–35 minutes or until golden brown and the juices run clear when the thickest part is pierced to the bone. Remove from the oven.

Preheat the oil in a deep fryer set to 190°C (375°F). Fry the wings in batches for a few minutes to crisp them. Drain on a plate lined with paper towels/kitchen paper and season to taste with salt. Serve with Dijon-Blue Cheese Dipping Sauce.

For the apple sauce

4 green apples, peeled, cored and chopped
60ml/¼ cup caster/white granulated sugar
½ teaspoon ground cinnamon
175 ml/¾ cup water

For the breakfast sausages

15 g/1 tablespoon butter
1 sweet apple, peeled, cored and chopped
1 onion, finely chopped
1 teaspoon fennel seeds
700g/1½ lb. minced/ground chicken breast
1½ tablespoons fresh sage, chopped
½ tablespoon soft light brown sugar
1–2 teaspoons olive oil
sea salt and freshly ground black pepper

For the pancakes

200g/1½ cups plain/all-purpose flour
2 tablespoons caster/white granulated sugar
2 teaspoons baking powder
½ teaspoon bicarbonate of soda/ baking soda
½ teaspoon sea salt
300–360 ml/1¼–1½ cups milk
2 eggs, beaten
30 g/2 tablespoons butter, melted
olive oil, to grease the pan

To serve

pure maple syrup

SERVES 4

'Chicks in a Blanket'
with apple sauce & maple syrup

'Pigs in a blanket' is a slang term for pancakes wrapped around breakfast sausages. They are the holy-grail brunch item for many!

For the apple sauce, combine the apples, sugar and cinnamon with the water in a saucepan or pot over a medium heat. Cover and cook over medium heat for 15–20 minutes or until the apples are soft. Allow to cool, then mash until smooth with a fork or potato masher. Set aside .

For the chicken-apple breakfast sausages, heat a small non-stick frying pan/skillet over medium a heat. Add the butter and melt. Add the apple and onion and season with a little salt, pepper and fennel seeds. Gently cook the mixture for 5–7 minutes to soften. When cooked, remove from heat and set aside. Heat a large non-stick frying pan/skillet over a medium-high heat. Place the chicken in a bowl and season well with salt and pepper, add the sage, sugar and olive oil. Add the apple, onion and fennel seed mixture, and mix with your hands. Using floured hands, divide the mixture and shape into 12 even sausages. Cook the sausages in the frying pan/skillet for 3–4 minutes, then flip and cook for another 2–4 minutes, until cooked through. Remove from the pan, set aside.

For the pancakes, in a bowl, mix together the dry ingredients and make a well in the centre. Start with 300 ml/1¼ cups milk, adding up to another 60 ml/¼ cup if necessary, as you mix with the flour. Add the beaten eggs and melted butter, combining with a whisk until well-mixed but still a bit lumpy.

Heat a frying pan/skillet and add a little oil. When hot, pour in a ladleful of pancake mix at a time. When the pancake starts to bubble on top and is turning golden brown on the underside, turn it and continue cooking until both sides are golden brown. Repeat the process with the remaining batter until you have 12 pancakes. Keep the cooked pancakes covered with a clean tea towel/kitchen cloth, to keep them warm while you finish cooking the rest. Once all pancakes are cooked, wrap around the sausages to form a roll, sausages in the middle. Serve with maple syrup and apple sauce.

For the marinated wings
140 g/1 cup plain/all-purpose flour
½ teaspoon paprika
½ teaspoon cayenne pepper
½ teaspoon sea salt
20 chicken wings, halved at the joints, tips removed

For the ranch dressing
250 ml/1 cup buttermilk, shaken
60 g/¼ cup mayonnaise
3 tablespoons sour cream
3 tablespoons freshly chopped flat-leaf parsley
2 tablespoons chives, finely chopped
4 teaspoons white wine vinegar or lemon juice
1 garlic clove, crushed
¼ teaspoon garlic powder
½ teaspoon sea salt, plus extra if needed
2 pinches of freshly ground black pepper

For the hot sauce
115 g/½ cup butter
120 ml/½ cup Louisiana hot sauce, or other hot pepper sauce
2 pinches of freshly ground black pepper
3 pinches of garlic powder
vegetable oil, for frying

To serve
celery and carrot sticks, for dipping

a sterilized, 500-ml/2-cup jar with a tight-fitting lid

MAKES 20

Buffalo bingo wings with homemade ranch dressing

Taking their name from the city in which they originated – Buffalo, New York – Buffalo wings have become an American staple, often served during sporting events or at late-night bars.

Combine the flour, paprika, cayenne pepper and salt in a large resealable plastic bag. Shake the bag to combine the spices. Next, put the chicken wings in the bag, seal tightly and shake them to coat evenly in the spice mix. Place the bag in the fridge for 60–90 minutes.

Place all of the ranch dressing ingredients into the jar. Seal tightly and shake to evenly distribute all the ingredients. Taste and season with additional salt and pepper Refrigerate until chilled and the flavours have melded, about 1 hour. The dressing lasts up to 3 days in the fridge.

For the hot sauce, combine the butter, Louisiana or other hot pepper sauce, ground black pepper and garlic powder in a small saucepan over a low heat. Warm until the butter is melted and the ingredients are well blended. Set aside.

In a large, deep, frying pan/skillet, add the vegetable oil to a depth of 2.5–5 cm/1–2 inches and heat to 190°C (375°F) or until the oil is bubbling steadily. Alternatively, use a deep fryer and follow the manufacturer's instructions.

Put the wings into the heated oil and fry them for 10–15 minutes or until some parts of the wings begin to turn a golden to dark brown colour.

Remove the wings from the oil and drain on paper towels/kitchen paper for a few seconds. Place the wings in a large bowl. Add the hot sauce mixture and stir, tossing the wings to thoroughly coat them. Serve with the homemade ranch dressing, and the celery and carrot, if you like.

90 ml/⅓ cup balsamic vinegar
50 g/¼ cup sea salt
1 bay leaf
1 teaspoon each dried thyme, oregano
   and rosemary
1.5 litres/6½ cups water
1.8 kg/4 lb. chicken wings, halved
   at the joints, tips removed
7 garlic cloves, crushed
3 tablespoons olive oil
1 tablespoon freshly ground black pepper
2 teaspoons chilli/hot red pepper flakes,
   or to taste
50 g/¼ cup fine breadcrumbs
60 g/1 cup finely grated Parmesan cheese

For the homemade ketchup
500 g/18 oz. tomato purée/paste
120 ml/½ cup white wine vinegar
1 teaspoon garlic powder
1 tablespoon onion powder
2 tablespoons caster/white granulated sugar
2 tablespoons molasses or treacle
1 teaspoon sea salt
1 teaspoon mustard powder
⅛ teaspoon each of ground cinnamon,
   cloves, allspice and cayenne pepper
250 ml/1 cup water
1 teaspoon powdered chia seeds,
   for thickness (optional)

For the pizza dipping sauce
250 ml/1 cup passata/strained tomatoes
1 tablespoon Italian seasoning
2 teaspoons dried oregano
1 teaspoon garlic powder

2–3 baking sheets, lined with foil

SERVES 4–6

Baked parmesan wings

When baked, these wings have the flavour and crispiness of fried chicken, without the decadence of fried food. They are very versatile and can be enjoyed with a variety of dipping sauces.

If serving with Homemade Ketchup, prepare this either the night before or at least an hour before you begin making the wings. Put all the ingredients in a blender or food processor and blend well. Chill in the fridge overnight or for at least 2 hours before serving.

Preheat the oven to 230°C (450°F) Gas 7.

Combine the vinegar, salt, bay leaf, thyme, oregano and rosemary with the water in a large saucepan and bring to a boil. Add the chicken wings, return to the boil and cook for 15 minutes. Using a slotted spoon, transfer the wings to a cooling rack and allow to dry for 15 minutes.

If serving with the Pizza Dipping Sauce, prepare this whilst the wings dry on the cooling rack. Simmer the passata with the seasonings for about 20 minutes, then let cool before serving.

Mash the garlic with a pinch of salt in a pestle and mortar until smooth. Combine the mashed garlic, olive oil, black pepper and chilli flakes in a large bowl. Add the breadcrumbs, then the chicken wings and toss to coat. Sprinkle with half the cheese. Transfer to the prepared baking sheets and sprinkle with the remaining cheese.

Bake in the preheated oven for 20–25 minutes, until golden and the juices run clear when the thickest part is pierced to the bone.

Serve with Homemade Ketchup or Pizza Dipping Sauce.

Barbecue chicken fries

Chicken, barbecue sauce and fries often end up together on a plate, so this combo is obvious, but it's the addition of melted cheese that elevates it to new heights. A crowd-pleaser, for sure.

For the cheese sauce
50 g/3 tablespoons unsalted butter
60 g/4 tablespoons plain/
   all-purpose flour
550 ml/1 pint milk
½ teaspoon sea salt
150 g/1¼ cups crumbled
   Cheddar cheese
2 slices cooked pancetta or bacon,
   finely chopped
freshly ground black pepper

For the fries
3–4 large floury potatoes
vegetable or sunflower oil, for frying
sea salt flakes

For the topping
300 g/10½ oz. cooked boneless
   chicken meat, shredded
250 ml/1 cup store-bought barbecue
   sauce, plus more for drizzling
salt and freshly ground black pepper
300 g/3 cups grated/shredded
   Red Leicester cheese,
   or other orange mild cheese

a shallow baking dish

SERVES 4

First, make the cheese sauce. Melt the butter in a saucepan. Stir in the flour and cook, stirring constantly, for 1 minute. Pour in the milk in a steady stream, whisking constantly and continue whisking gently until the sauce begins to thicken, 3–5 minutes. Stir in the salt. Remove from the heat and add the cheese and chopped pancetta or bacon, mixing well with a spoon to incorporate. Taste and adjust the seasoning. Set aside.

Next, make the fries. Peel the potatoes and trim on all sides to get a block. Cut the block into slices about 1-cm/³⁄₈-inch thick, then cut again into fries. Put the potatoes into a bowl of iced water for at least 5 minutes, to remove any excess starch. Fill a large saucepan one-third full with the oil or, if using a deep fryer, follow the manufacturer's instructions. Heat the oil to 190°C (375°F) or until a cube of bread browns in 30 seconds. Drain the potatoes and dry very well. Working in batches, fry a handful of potatoes at a time. Place the potatoes in a frying basket (or use a slotted metal spoon) and lower into the hot oil carefully. Fry for 4 minutes. Remove and drain on paper towels/kitchen paper. Repeat until all of the potatoes have been fried.

Just before serving, skim any debris off the top of the cooking oil and reheat to the same temperature. Fry as before, in batches, but only cook until almost crisp and golden, as they will be baked to melt the cheese. This should take less than 2 minutes. Remove and drain on paper towels/kitchen paper. Repeat until all of the potatoes have been fried. Sprinkle with the salt flakes.

Meanwhile, in a saucepan, combine the shredded chicken and barbecue sauce and warm over a low heat. Taste and adjust the seasoning. Set aside and keep warm. Warm the cheese sauce in another small saucepan. Set aside and keep warm. Preheat the oven to 200°C (400°F) Gas 6. Spread the fries in the baking dish. Scatter the cheese and return to the oven to melt, about 5 minutes. Remove from oven and add the warm cheese sauce and chicken. Drizzle with extra barbecue sauce and serve.

Barbecue chicken &
two cheeses mac 'n' cheese

Ideal for hectic households, this straightforward combination has tastes that appeal to all generations, with the added bonus of being very quick to prepare. Serve with corn, coleslaw and a crisp green salad to go with the barbecue flavours.

a handful of coarse sea salt
500 g/1 lb. 2 oz. macaroni
250 g/4 oz. skinless and boneless poached
  or roasted chicken, shredded
250 ml/1 cup store-bought barbecue sauce
250 g/8 oz. mozzarella cheese, half grated/
  shredded and half sliced
50 g/1 cup fresh breadcrumbs

For the béchamel sauce
50 g/3½ tablespoons unsalted butter
60 g/6 tablespoons plain/all-purpose flour
625 ml/2½ cups milk
200 g/1⅔ cups grated/shredded Cheddar cheese
sea salt and freshly ground black pepper

a baking dish

SERVES 6–8

Bring a large saucepan of water to a boil. Add the coarse sea salt, then let the water return to a rolling boil. Add the macaroni, stir well and cook according to the package instructions until very tender. Stir periodically to prevent the macaroni from sticking together. When cooked, drain, rinse well under running water and let drip dry in a colander.

Put the shredded chicken and the barbecue sauce in a large bowl and mix well. Taste and adjust the seasoning. Set aside.

Preheat the grill/broiler to medium.

To make the béchamel sauce, melt the butter in a saucepan. Stir in the flour and cook, stirring constantly, for 1 minute. Pour in the milk in a steady stream, whisking constantly, and continue to whisk for 3–5 minutes until the sauce begins to thicken. Season with sea salt. Remove from the heat and add the cheese, mixing well with a spoon to incorporate. Taste and adjust the seasoning.

Put the cooked macaroni in a large mixing bowl. Pour over the hot béchamel sauce and the chicken mixture and mix well. Taste and adjust the seasoning.

Transfer the macaroni to a baking dish and spread evenly. Top with the sliced mozzarella cheese and a good grinding of black pepper and sprinkle the breadcrumbs evenly over the top. Grill/broil for 5–10 minutes until the top is crunchy and golden brown. Serve immediately.

Chicken alfredo mac 'n' cheese

Somewhat retro in feel, creamy alfredo sauce flavoured with parsley lends itself well to mac 'n' cheese. Shredded, skinless roast chicken pieces give this dish a lovely, chunky texture, but cooked minced/ground chicken also works well with the shape of the macaroni, so can just as easily be used.

a handful of coarse sea salt

500 g/1 lb. 2 oz. macaroni

2 tablespoons vegetable oil

1 large onion, diced

500 g/1 lb. 2 oz. skinless and boneless poached or roasted chicken, shredded

a small bunch of fresh flat-leaf parsley, finely chopped

For the béchamel sauce

50 g/3½ tablespoons unsalted butter

60 g/6 tablespoons plain/all-purpose flour

625 ml/2½ cups milk

100 g/1¼ cups grated Parmesan cheese

200 g/1⅔ cups grated/shredded Cheddar cheese

50 g/1 cup fresh breadcrumbs

sea salt and freshly ground black pepper

a baking dish

SERVES 6–8

Bring a large saucepan of water to a boil. Add the coarse sea salt, then let the water return to a rolling boil. Add the macaroni, stir well and cook according to the package instructions until very tender. Stir periodically to prevent the macaroni from sticking together. When cooked, drain, rinse well under running water and let drip dry in a colander.

Heat the oil in a large frying pan/skillet. Add the onion and cook over high heat for about 5 minutes until brown and caramelized, stirring occasionally. Add the chicken and cook for 5–7 minutes more until just browned, stirring occasionally. Taste and adjust the seasoning. Set aside.

Preheat the grill/broiler to medium.

To make the béchamel sauce, melt the butter in a saucepan. Stir in the flour and cook, stirring constantly, for 1 minute. Pour in the milk in a steady stream, whisking constantly, and continue to whisk for 3–5 minutes until the sauce begins to thicken. Season with sea salt. Remove from the heat and add the cheeses, mixing well with a spoon to incorporate. Taste and adjust the seasoning.

Put the cooked macaroni in a large mixing bowl. Pour over the hot béchamel sauce and mix well, then stir in the chicken mixture. Taste and adjust the seasoning. Transfer the macaroni mixture to a baking dish and spread evenly. Top with a good grinding of black pepper, scatter over the parsley and sprinkle the breadcrumbs evenly over the top.

Grill/broil for 5–10 minutes until the top is crunchy and golden brown. Serve immediately.

Fun in a Bun

Chicken Caesar sliders wrapped in Parma ham with Caesar dressing

These cute sliders combine all the ingredients of a chicken Caesar salad. They're light and delicious and make great canapés to serve at parties – perfect for entertaining.

For the Caesar dressing

1 egg yolk
1 garlic clove, crushed
2 anchovy fillets in oil, drained and chopped
1 tablespoon lemon juice, freshly squeezed
1 teaspoon Worcestershire sauce
150 ml/^{2}/$_3$ cup olive oil
25 g/1 oz. Parmesan cheese, finely
   grated/shredded
sea salt and freshly ground black pepper

For the sliders

200 g/7 oz. lean minced/ground chicken
   or turkey
6 chives, finely chopped
1 teaspoon anchovy paste
20g/^{3}/$_4$ oz. Parmesan cheese, finely
   grated/shredded
1 teaspoon beaten egg
a pinch of sea salt
a pinch of freshly ground black pepper
2 slices Parma ham, cut in half

To serve

4 seeded mini rolls
a handful of Romano lettuce leaves

a sterilized screw-top jar with a tight-fitting lid
4 cocktail sticks/toothpicks

MAKES 4 SLIDERS

Preheat the oven to 180°C (350°F) Gas 4.

To make the Caesar dressing, whisk the egg yolk in a small bowl with the garlic, anchovies, lemon juice, Worcestershire sauce and salt and pepper, to taste, until frothy. Gradually whisk in the olive oil a little at a time until thick and glossy. Add 2 tablespoons of water to thin the dressing and stir in the Parmesan cheese. Store in the fridge in a sterilized screw-top jar and use on the same day as it was made.

To make the sliders, put the chicken in a bowl with the chives, anchovy paste, Parmesan cheese, egg and salt and pepper. Work together with your hands until evenly mixed. Divide the mixture into quarters and shape into 4 slider patties. Press each slider down to make the patties nice and flat.

Wrap a piece of Parma ham around each slider and lay them on a baking sheet. Bake the sliders in the preheated oven for 15–20 minutes until cooked through.

Cut each of the rolls in half and put a Romano lettuce leaf on the bottom half of each roll. Top each with a cooked slider, drizzle with Caesar dressing and finish with the lids of the rolls. Put a cocktail stick/toothpick through the middle of each slider to hold it in place and serve whilst hot.

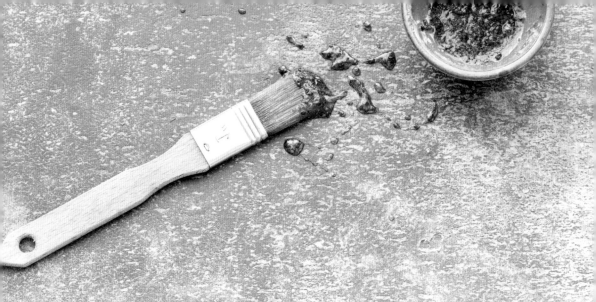

Chicken panini with Gouda, red onion & honey-mustard dressing

When melted, Dutch Gouda cheese becomes velvety and gooey, making it the ideal cheese for panini.

1 ciabatta loaf
2 tablespoons store-bought honey-mustard dressing, plus extra to serve
1 cooked chicken breast
8 thinly sliced rings of red onion
2 handfuls of rocket/arugula
80 g/3 oz. Gouda cheese, sliced
vegetable oil, for brushing

a panini press

MAKES 2 PANINI

Preheat a panini press. Cut the top and bottom off the ciabatta so that it is about 3-cm/1-inch high. Save the crusts for another use. Slice open lengthways and then cut in half.

Spread the honey-mustard dressing on the inside of both sandwiches.

Slice the chicken into 4 pieces lengthways. Layer the fillings in the 2 sandwiches starting with the chicken, followed by the onion and rocket, finishing with the cheese. Brush both sides of the panini with oil and toast in the preheated panini press for 3 minutes, or according to the manufacturer's instructions. The bread should be golden brown and the filling warmed through.

Serve with extra honey-mustard dressing on the side for dipping.

Chicken panini with Scamorza, tomato & watercress

Scamorza is smoked mozzarella cheese. It has a more pronounced flavour and firmer texture than the fresh variety. Sun-blush tomatoes can be subsituted for the roasted tomatoes if you are short of time.

1 ciabatta loaf
1 cooked chicken breast
4 slices roasted tomatoes
2 handfuls of watercress
80 g/3 oz. Scamorza cheese, sliced
vegetable oil, for brushing

a panini press

MAKES 2 PANINI

Preheat a panini press. Cut the top and bottom off the ciabatta so that it is about 3-cm/1-inch high. Save the crusts for another use. Slice open lengthways and then cut in half.

Slice the chicken into 4 pieces lengthways. Layer 2 slices on each sandwich and follow with the tomatoes, watercress and then the cheese. Brush both sides of the panini with oil and toast in the preheated panini press for 3 minutes, or according to the manufacturer's instructions. The bread should be golden brown and the filling warmed through. Serve immediately.

Thai chicken burger with mango, crispy shallots & sweet chilli dressing

A lovely homemade sweet chilli/chile dressing adds that classic Thai hot, sweet, salty and sour flavour we all love and is a perfect foil to the chicken and mango.

1 tablespoon peanut or vegetable oil,
    plus extra for cooking
1 shallot, thinly sliced
1 garlic clove, crushed
2.5-cm/1-inch piece of fresh ginger, grated
1 teaspoons shrimp paste
    (from Thai and Asian food stores)
1 tablespoon desiccated/shredded coconut
1 teaspoon caster/white granulated sugar
500 g/1 lb. 2 oz. skinless, boneless chicken
    thigh fillets, roughly chopped

For the sweet chilli/ chile dressing

1 chilli/chile, deseeded and sliced
juice of 2 limes, freshly squeezed
1 tablespoon Thai fish sauce
2 tablespoons caster/white granulated sugar

To serve

4 rolls
a handful of Asian salad leaves
a handful of fresh herbs (e.g. Thai basil,
    coriander/cilantro, mint)
1 mango, peeled, stoned and sliced
2 tablespoons crispy fried shallots

a ridged stovetop grill pan

SERVES 4

Heat the oil in a wok and gently fry the shallot, garlic and ginger for 5 minutes until softened. Stir in the shrimp paste, coconut and sugar and stir-fry for 1 minute until fragrant, then continue to stir until you have a slightly sticky paste mix. Set aside to let cool.

Place the chicken pieces in a food processor with the cooled spice paste and blend until coarsely minced. Shape into 8 small burger patties. Press each burger down to make them nice and flat, then cover and chill for 30 minutes.

Meanwhile, make the chilli dressing. Place the ingredients in a bowl and whisk until the sugar is dissolved.

Heat a ridged stovetop grill pan over a high heat. Brush the patties with a little oil and cook for 3–4 minutes on each side until charred and cooked through. Rest for 5 minutes.

To serve, cut the rolls almost in half and open out wide. Fill with salad leaves and herbs. Top each roll with 2 burgers and a few mango slices. Drizzle over the dressing and scatter over the crispy shallots. Serve at once.

Creole spiced chicken burger

Creole cooking is mainly associated with the southern United States and the Mississippi Delta, where traditions of French, Spanish and African foods combine. Ready-made spice mixes are available from supermarkets and specialist food shops.

700 g/1 lb. 9 oz. skinless, boneless chicken
    breasts, coarsely chopped
1 tablespoon water
50 g/1 cup fresh white breadcrumbs
zest of 1 lime, freshly grated
2 teaspoons Creole seasoning
2–3 tablespoons plain/all-purpose flour,
    seasoned with sea salt and freshly ground
    black pepper
2 eggs, lightly beaten
100 g/⅔ cup medium polenta/cornmeal
sea salt and freshly ground black pepper
sunflower oil, for shallow frying

For the creole salsa
2 tomatoes, chopped
½ a red onion, finely chopped
1 jalapeño chilli/chile, deseeded and
    finely chopped
juice of 1 lime, freshly squeezed
1 tablespoon freshly chopped coriander/cilantro

To serve
2 burger buns, halved
100 g/3-3½ cups shredded cos/romaine lettuce
4 tablespoons mayonnaise
store-bought barbecue sauce (optional)

SERVES 4

Put the chicken and water in a food processor and pulse until just minced. Add the breadcrumbs, lime zest, Creole seasoning and some salt and pepper and pulse until smooth. Transfer the mixture to a bowl, cover and chill for 30 minutes.

Divide the mixture into 8 portions and shape into patties. Dust the patties lightly with seasoned flour, then dip them first into the egg and then the cornmeal to coat thoroughly.

Heat a shallow layer of oil in a non-stick frying pan/skillet and when hot, add the patties and fry for 3 minutes on each side until golden and cooked through. Drain on kitchen paper/paper towels and keep them warm.

Meanwhile, to make the salsa, put the tomatoes, onion, chilli, lime juice and coriander in a bowl and season to taste with salt and pepper. Mix well and set aside until required.

Lightly toast the buns, top each half with shredded lettuce, 2 patties, some mayonnaise, the salsa and some barbecue sauce, if using. Serve hot.

Chicken burger with herb mayonnaise

This is a delicious and light burger. Don't overwork the mixture as you process it – use the pulse button and blend briefly, checking the mixture each time before processing again.

For the herb mayo

3 egg yolks

2 teaspoons Dijon mustard

2 teaspoons white wine vinegar
　　or lemon juice, freshly squeezed

½ teaspoon sea salt

300 ml/2 cups olive oil

a handful of any fresh green herbs, such as
　　basil, flat-leaf parsley or tarragon, chopped

MAKES ABOUT 400 ML/2 CUPS

For the burger

750 g/1 lb 10 oz. skinless, boneless chicken
　　breasts, minced/ground

1 tablespoon milk

1 onion, finely chopped

2 garlic cloves, crushed

sea salt and freshly ground black pepper

olive oil, for brushing

To serve

4 sesame seed buns, halved

4 tablespoons Herb Mayo, plus extra to serve

a handful of baby spinach leaves

2 tomatoes, sliced

SERVES 4

First, make the herb mayo. Put the egg yolks, mustard, vinegar or lemon juice and salt in a food processor and blend until foaming. With the blade running, gradually pour in the oil through a funnel until thick and glossy. Add the herbs to the food processor and blend until the sauce is speckled green. If it is too thick, add a little water. Then adjust the seasoning to taste. Use as required. Any leftovers can be kept in the fridge for up to 3 days.

Put the chicken, milk, onion, garlic and some salt and pepper in a food processor and pulse until smooth. Transfer the mixture to a bowl, cover and chill for 30 minutes.

Preheat the barbecue or grill/broiler.

Divide the mixture into 4 portions and, using wet hands, shape into burger patties. Press each burger down to make them nice and flat. Brush the patties lightly with olive oil and barbecue or grill/broil for 5–6 minutes on each side until cooked through. Test one by inserting a metal skewer into the centre – it should feel hot to the touch when the patty is cooked. Keep them warm.

Lightly toast the buns under the grill/broiler or in the toaster and spread the top halves with herb mayo. Fill the buns with spinach leaves, patties and tomato slices and serve with extra herb mayo.

Deep-fried buttermilk chicken burger

'Nduja is a type of Italian salami blended with roasted red peppers into a spicy paste. If you are unable to find it, you can simply blend some chorizo sausage in a food processor until it is paste-like, which makes for a decent alternative.

8 skinless, boneless chicken thighs
250 ml/1 cup buttermilk
sunflower oil, for frying

For the slaw
125 g/2 cups shredded red cabbage
100 g/³⁄₄ cup grated/shredded carrots
½ red onion, thinly sliced
1 teaspoon sea salt
1½ teaspoons caster/white granulated sugar
2 teaspoons white wine vinegar
6 tablespoons mayonnaise

For the coating
100 g/³⁄₄ cup plain/all-purpose flour
1 teaspoon sea salt
1 teaspoon mustard powder
½ teaspoon smoked paprika
½ teaspoon celery salt
¼ teaspoon freshly ground black pepper

To serve
4 brioche burger buns
125 g/4 oz. 'nduja sausage
a handful of lettuce leaves

SERVES 4

Cut the chicken thigh fillets in half and place in a shallow dish. Pour over the buttermilk, cover and chill overnight. This will tenderize the chicken. The next day, remove the chicken from the fridge and return to room temperature for 30 minutes.

Make the slaw. Combine the cabbage, carrots and onion with the salt, sugar and vinegar and set aside for 30 minutes. Drain the cabbage mixture and combine with the mayonnaise.

Preheat the oven to 180°C (350°F) Gas 4.

Make the coating mix. In a bowl, combine the flour with the salt, mustard powder, smoked paprika, celery salt and black pepper.

Carefully remove the chicken thighs from the buttermilk and immediately dip into the flour mixture, making sure they are completely coated.

Heat 5 cm/2 inches of sunflower oil in a saucepan to 190°C (375°F) or until a cube of bread browns in 30 seconds. Deep-fry the coated chicken pieces for 3–4 minutes on each side until crisp and golden. Transfer them to the oven to keep warm while cooking the rest.

To serve, cut the buns in half and lightly toast the cut sides under the grill/broiler. Fill with the chicken fritters and add some 'nduja, lettuce and slaw. Serve at once, with Sweet Potato Fries, if you like (see page 30).

Chicken steak & bacon burger with Caesar dressing

Caesar salad is as much an American icon as a burger and here the two combine perfectly in a great sourdough sandwich. You can add a poached egg to the filling, if you like.

4 small skinless, boneless chicken breasts
4 slices smoked bacon
sea salt and freshly ground black pepper

To serve
Caesar Dressing (see page 53)
8 slices sourdough bread
1 cos/romaine lettuce heart, leaves separated
25 g/1 oz. Parmesan cheese, pared
 into shavings
olive oil, for brushing

a ridged stovetop grill pan

SERVES 4

Lay the chicken breast fillets flat on a chopping board and, using a sharp knife, cut horizontally through the thickest part but don't cut all the way through. Open the fillets out flat. Brush with olive oil and season with salt and pepper.

Preheat a ridged stovetop grill pan until hot and cook the chicken fillets for 3–4 minutes on each side until cooked through. Keep them warm. Cook the bacon on the hot grill pan for 2–3 minutes until cooked to your liking. Keep it warm.

Toast the sourdough on the grill pan until lightly charred. Meanwhile, prepare the Caesar dressing (see page 53.)

Spread each slice of sourdough with a little Caesar dressing and top half of them with lettuce, chicken, bacon and Parmesan cheese shavings. Finish with a second slice of sourdough and serve.

Open chicken burger
with grilled vegetables

This open-faced sandwich is full of the flavours of Mediterranean cooking,
with char-grilled vegetables, focaccia bread and salty olive tapenade.

750 g/1 lb. 10 oz. skinless, boneless chicken
   breasts, minced
2 garlic cloves, crushed
1 tablespoon freshly chopped rosemary
zest and juice of 1 lemon, freshly squeezed
   and grated
1 egg yolk
50 g/2 oz. dried breadcrumbs
1 aubergine/eggplant
2 courgettes/zucchini

For the tapenade
125 g/1¼ cups black olives, pitted
2 anchovies in oil, drained
1 garlic clove, crushed
2 tablespoons capers, rinsed
1 teaspoon Dijon mustard
4 tablespoons extra virgin olive oil

To serve
4 slices focaccia
radicchio or rocket/arugula leaves
sea salt and freshly ground black pepper
olive oil, for brushing

SERVES 4

To make the tapenade, put the olives, anchovies, garlic, capers, mustard and oil in a food processor and blend to form a fairly smooth paste. Season to taste with black pepper. Transfer to a dish, cover and store in the fridge for up to 5 days.

Put the chicken, garlic, rosemary, lemon zest and juice, egg yolk, breadcrumbs and some salt and pepper in a food processor and pulse until smooth. Transfer the mixture to a bowl, cover and chill for 30 minutes. Divide the mixture into 4 portions and shape into patties.

Preheat the barbecue or grill/broiler.

Cut the aubergine into 12 slices and the courgettes into 12 thin strips. Brush with olive oil and season with salt and pepper. Barbecue or grill the vegetables for 2–3 minutes on each side until charred and softened. Keep them warm.

Meanwhile, brush the chicken patties lightly with olive oil and barbecue or grill/broil for 5 minutes on each side until charred and cooked through. Keep them warm.

Toast the focaccia and top each slice with radicchio or rocket leaves, patties, grilled vegetables and some tapenade. Serve immediately.

4 boneless chicken thighs, skin on
250 ml/1 cup buttermilk
3½ teaspoons chilli/hot red
    pepper flakes
1¼ tablespoons cayenne pepper
1 tablespoon sea salt
130 g/1 cup plain/all-purpose flour
½ tablespoon garlic powder
2 eggs
½ tablespoon apple cider vinegar
40 g/½ cup fresh breadcrumbs
35g/¼ cup stone-ground yellow grits
    or polenta
rapeseed/canola oil, for deep-frying

For the sage biscuits

260 g/2 cups plain/all-purpose flour,
    plus extra for dusting
¼ teaspoon bicarbonate
    of soda/baking soda
1 tablespoon baking powder
1 teaspoon sea salt, plus extra
    to season
a small bunch of sage,
    thinly shredded
85 g/6 tablespoons unsalted butter,
    very cold, cubed
250 ml/1 cup buttermilk
60g/¼ cup butter, melted,
    for brushing

To serve

runny honey, for drizzling
2 large dill pickles, sliced
store-bought southern style gravy

a 7.5-cm/3-inch round plain
    cookie cutter

MAKES 12

Fried chicken
& biscuit sliders

These sliders use chicken thighs and are the epitome of a breakfast
in the southern states of the US.

The night before you'd like to make these sliders, cut the chicken
into 12 bite-sized pieces. Combine in a bag with the buttermilk, chilli
flakes, cayenne pepper and salt. Seal and refrigerate overnight. The
next day, heat 5 cm/2 inches oil in a frying pan/skillet or a deep-
fryer to 180°C (350°F). In one bowl, combine half the flour with
the garlic powder. In another, whisk together eggs and vinegar.
In another bowl combine the remaining flour, breadcrumbs and
grits. Once the oil is hot, take the chicken, 2 or 3 pieces at a time,
from the buttermilk and shake the excess buttermilk off. Dredge
in the flour mixture, then in the eggs, and then in the flour and
breadcrumbs. Make sure the chicken is completely coated in the
third mixture and then drop into the hot oil. Fry for 3–5 minutes
until golden brown, crisp and cooked through. Transfer onto
a rack to cool. Repeat until all of the chicken is fried.

Preheat the oven to 230°C (450°F) Gas 8.

To make the sage biscuits, combine the dry ingredients and sage
in a bowl, or in the bowl of a food processor. Add the butter and
cut into flour until it resembles coarse meal. Handle the dough
as little as possible. Add the buttermilk and mix just until combined.
It should be very wet. Turn the dough out onto a floured board.
Gently, gently pat the dough out until it's about 1 cm/½ inch
thick. Fold the dough about 5 times, then gently press the dough
down to 2.5 cm/1 inch thick. Use the cutter to cut the dough into
12 rounds. Place the biscuits on a baking sheet. Brush the tops with
melted butter and season lightly with salt. Bake in the preheated
oven for 10–12 minutes, until light golden brown on top and bottom.

Meanwhile, prepare the gravy according to packet instructions and
keep hot. When you are ready to serve, halve the warm biscuits and
smear generously with honey. Place a fried chicken bite and a dill
pickle slice on each one and serve, with the hot gravy on the side
for spooning.

Tandoori chicken grilled cheese
with paneer & mango chutney

The taste of this sandwich depends entirely on the mango chutney, so use the best one you can find. Something with a bit of ginger and apple, although less traditional, partners the melted cheese amazingly well. A spoonful of apple sauce (see page 38) can be added to ordinary chutney if desired. Some raita, in a small dish, is delightful for dipping.

2 skinless, boneless chicken breasts

4–5 tablespoons tandoori paste

2 large naan breads

unsalted butter, softened

2 thin slices mild cheese, such as Gouda or Fontina cheese

4–6 tablespoons store-bought mango chutney, plus extra to serve

100 g/scant cup grated/shredded paneer cheese

sea salt

For the raita

250 ml/1 cup natural/plain yogurt

½ cucumber, finely chopped

a handful of fresh mint, chopped

a large of pinch sea salt

SERVES 2

Heat the oven to 180°C (350°F) Gas 4. Coat the chicken liberally with the tandoori paste, season lightly with salt and bake until cooked through, 20–25 minutes. Let cool then slice into thin, even pieces.

While the chicken is cooking, prepare the raita dip, by squeezing any excess moisture from the cucumber with paper towels/kitchen paper and then mixing together all of the ingredients thoroughly. Set aside.

Butter the naan breads on one side and set aside.

This is easiest if assembled in a large heavy-based non-stick frying pan/skillet. You'll need to cook the sandwiches in 2 batches, as naan breads are fairly large. Put one slice of bread in the pan/skillet, butter-side down. You will need to fold the bread over to form a sandwich, so position the filling on one side. Put one slice of cheese on the naan, then arrange half the chicken slices over the top. Drop spoonfuls of the chutney on top then spread the spoonfuls out, gently and evenly. Sprinkle with half of the paneer. Fold one half of the bread over the top of the other half to cover.

Turn the heat to medium and cook the first side until deep golden for 3–5 minutes, pressing gently with a spatula. Carefully turn with a large spatula and cook on the second side, for 2–3 minutes more or until deep golden brown all over.

Remove from the pan/skillet and transfer to a plate with the raita alongside. Let cool for a few minutes before serving. Repeat the cooking instructions for the remaining sandwich.

Chipotle chicken grilled cheese
with roasted green peppers & queso fresco

If poblano peppers are available, use them here instead of the green (bell) peppers for a more authentic touch of southwestern spice.

2 tablespoons vegetable oil

1 chipotle chilli/chile in adobo sauce, finely chopped, plus 1 teaspoon sauce

juice of 1 lime, freshly squeezed

2 skinless, boneless chicken breasts

a pinch of sea salt

1 green (bell) pepper, deseeded and thinly sliced

1 round brown loaf, cut in half widthways and lengthways to form 4 triangular slices

unsalted butter, softened

2 thin slices mild cheese, such as Gouda or Fontina

100 g/¾ cup crumbled queso fresco or feta cheese

a small handful of fresh coriander/cilantro, finely chopped

SERVES 2

Pre-heat the oven to 180°C (350°F) Gas 4.

In a small bowl, combine 1 tablespoon of the vegetable oil with the chilli and lime juice and mix well. Coat the chicken breasts with this mixture, season with salt and bake until cooked through, 20–25 minutes. Let cool, then slice thinly.

Meanwhile, combine the remaining oil and (bell) pepper strips in a small non-stick frying pan/skillet and cook until softened and lightly charred. Set aside.

Butter all the bread slices on one side and set aside.

This is easiest if assembled in a large non-stick frying pan/skillet. Unless you have a really large pan/skillet, you'll need to cook these sandwiches in batches. Put one slice of bread in the pan/skillet, butter-side down. Put one slice of cheese on top, then spread half of the chicken slices on top of the cheese. Arrange half the pepper strips on top and sprinkle with half of the crumbled cheese and coriander. Cover with another bread slice, butter side up.

Turn the heat to medium and cook the first side for 4–5 minutes until deep golden, pressing gently with a spatula. Carefully turn with a large spatula and cook on the second side, for 2–3 minutes more or until deep golden brown all over.

Remove from the pan/skillet, transfer to a plate and let cool for a few minutes before serving. Repeat for the remaining sandwich.

Chipotle chicken & rajas tacos

Rajas simply means strips of (bell) pepper. Roast chicken works best in this Mexican-inspired recipe and makes for a delicious meal.

500 g/1 lb 2 oz. skinless, boneless chicken, thinkly sliced
2 teaspoons ground cumin
1 teaspoon chipotle chilli/chili powder
2 teaspoons sea salt
2 tablespoons vegetable oil

For the rajas
1 red (bell) pepper, deseeded and thinly sliced
1 yellow (bell) pepper, deseeded and thinly sliced
2 tablespoons vegetable oil
2 garlic cloves, crushed
1 teaspoon dried oregano
sea salt

To serve
6–8 corn or flour tortillas, warmed
sour cream
freshly ground black pepper
hot sauce (such as Tabasco)

SERVES 3–4

Preheat the oven to 180°C (350°F) Gas 4.

To prepare the rajas, put the peppers in a large roasting pan. Add the oil, garlic, oregano and salt and toss well. Spread evenly in the pan and roast in the preheated oven for 20–30 minutes until the peppers begin to char. Remove from the oven and set aside until needed. Do not turn off the oven.

Put the chicken in a roasting pan. Add the cumin, chilli powder, salt and oil and toss well. Spread in an even layer and roast for 15–20 minutes until browned and cooked through.

To serve, put a generous helping of sliced chicken in the middle of each tortilla. Top with rajas, a spoonful of sour cream and a good grinding of black pepper. Serve immediately with extra sour cream and any hot sauce on the side.

Chicken & chorizo quesadilla

Serve these for brunch, lunch or dinner, with rice and beans if a more substantial meal is required. The chicken can be prepared in advance to make this recipe even more speedy.

650 g/1 lb. 7 oz. skinless, boneless chicken
chicken or vegetable stock, or water,
    as required
2 tablespoons vegetable oil
1 onion, finely chopped
2 garlic cloves, crushed
1 teaspoon ground cumin
1 teaspoon dried oregano
1 teaspoon sea salt
1 fresh green chilli/chile, deseeded and
    finely chopped
70 g/2 oz. chorizo, finely chopped
1 x 400-g/14-oz. can chopped tomatoes
8 large flour tortillas
200 g/2 cups grated/shredded Cheddar
    or Monterey Jack cheese

To serve
sour cream
store-bought guacamole (or see page 90)

SERVES 4–6

Put the chicken in a saucepan and add enough stock or water to cover. If using water or unseasoned stock, season with salt. Bring to a boil over a medium heat, then cover and simmer for 30–40 minutes until cooked through. Remove from the pan and let cool, then shred the chicken using your hands or 2 forks. Taste and adjust the seasoning.

Preheat the oven to 120°C (250°F) Gas ½.

Heat 1 tablespoon of the oil in a saucepan over a medium-high heat. Add the onion and cook for 5–8 minutes, stirring occasionally, until golden. Add the garlic, cumin, oregano, salt, chilli and chorizo and cook for 1–2 minutes, stirring often. Stir in the tomatoes and cover. Simmer for 15 minutes then uncover and cook for 10–20 minutes until reduced. Stir in the shredded chicken.

To assemble the quesadillas, spread a quarter of the chicken mixture on 4 of the tortillas. Sprinkle each with a quarter of the cheese and top with another tortilla.

Heat the remaining oil in a non-stick frying pan/skillet set over a medium heat. When hot, add a quesadilla, lower the heat and cook for 2–3 minutes until golden on one side and the cheese begins to melt. Turn over and cook the other side for 2–3 minutes. Transfer to a heatproof plate and keep warm in the preheated oven while you cook the rest.

To serve, top each quesadilla with sour cream and guacamole. Cut into wedges and serve immediately.

Spicy & Saucy

Vietnamese chicken salad *with hot mint*

This salad is so tasty and fresh, especially with the sharp onion pickle. Enjoy with plenty of the dipping sauce on a hot summer's day.

For the onion pickle
1 red onion, thinly sliced
3 tablespoons cider vinegar
1 tablespoon caster/white
   granulated sugar
a pinch of sea salt
a pinch of freshly ground
   black pepper

For the salad
1.2 litres/5 cups water
3 chicken thighs, skin on and bone in
1 chicken stock cube
200 g/1¼ cups basmati rice
1 knob of butter
1 garlic clove, crushed
10 sprigs of hot mint
   (or Thai sweet basil), chopped
a small handful of fresh coriander/
   cilantro, stalk on, chopped
a pinch of freshly ground
   black pepper

For the dipping sauce
2 tablespoons fish sauce
2 teaspoons caster/white
   granulated sugar
2-cm/1-inch piece of fresh
   ginger, grated
1 bird's eye chilli/chile, deseeded
   and finely chopped
1 garlic clove, crushed
1 tablespoon cider vinegar

SERVES 2–3

Start by making the onion pickle. Set aside about one-fifth of the onion slices. Combine the remainder with the other ingredients and leave for at least 1 hour.

Next, start the salad. Put the water and the chicken thighs in a saucepan over a medium heat and cover with a lid. Bring to a boil, then skim off the scum from the surface with a spoon. Add the stock cube and cook for around 25–30 minutes (you will need to extract some of the stock 20 minutes into cooking, see the instruction below).

Wash and drain the rice. Finely chop the reserved portion of red onion. Melt the butter in a non-stick saucepan over a low heat and fry the onion and garlic. Add the rice and stir it to coat it in the flavours. Once the chicken has been poaching in the other pan for 20 minutes, take out 350 ml/1½ cups of the poaching stock and pour it into the pan of rice with a pinch of salt. Cover with a lid and raise the heat to medium; this technique will cook the rice by steaming it. When the liquid comes to a boil, turn the heat back down to low and continue to cook for 15–20 minutes, stirring occasionally.

To make the dipping sauce, mix the ingredients together in a bowl with 2 tablespoons of the leftover chicken poaching stock. When the chicken has finished poaching, remove it from the pan and allow it to rest for 10 minutes while the rice is still cooking. Reserve the leftover stock for another time – allow it to cool completely, then refrigerate or freeze it.

Tear the meat from the chicken bones using your fingers or 2 forks. Discard the skin. Mix the chicken with the onion pickle (discarding the pickling juices), mint, coriander and pepper. Serve the salad at room temperature with the rice and dipping sauce.

Chicken tikka masala

Many polls have concluded that chicken tikka masala is the most popular dish in the UK and it's also a much-loved Indian dish in the USA. It's a great one to batch-cook and portion, too, and it's delicious cold for lunch.

4 teaspoons olive oil
1 red onion, diced
1 garlic clove, crushed
4 skinless, boneless chicken breasts
    (or 2 breasts and 2 boneless thighs), diced
1 red chilli/chile, deseeded and finely chopped
a pinch each of ground ginger, ground
    turmeric, ground cumin and paprika
juice of ½ lime, freshly squeezed
    (the rest can be cut for serving)
3 tablespoons tomato purée/paste
a large pinch of fresh coriander/cilantro,
    chopped, plus extra whole leaves to garnish
1 teaspoon soft dark brown sugar
1 x 200-g/7-oz. can chopped tomatoes
5 tablespoons double/heavy cream
sea salt and freshly ground black pepper

To serve
cooked basmati rice
naan bread

SERVES 4

Heat the oil in a frying pan/skillet set over a high heat and fry the onion and garlic for about 5 minutes until they start to brown. Add the diced chicken, the chilli, all the pinches of seasoning, a pinch of salt and pepper, and the lime juice. Stir in the tomato purée, coriander and sugar. Lastly, add the chopped tomatoes and double cream.

Bring to a boil, then reduce the heat to low and simmer for 15–20 minutes, until the chicken is cooked through. Taste and check the seasoning. Serve with rice and naan bread, and a sprinkling of extra whole coriander leaves.

Butter chicken

This popular chicken curry, natively called 'makhani' has its origins in the Mughal dynasty.
Remember to start this recipe the day before.

For the marinade

150 g/1¼ cups cashew nuts
1 tablespoon fennel seeds
2 teaspoons ground cinnamon
1 tablespoon ground coriander
1 teaspoon cardamom seeds, crushed
1 teaspoon black peppercorns
½ teaspoon ground cloves
4 garlic cloves, crushed
2 teaspoons freshly grated ginger
2 tablespoons white wine vinegar
100 g/3½ oz. tomato purée/paste
150 g/5¼ oz. natural/plain yogurt

For the curry

800 g/1¾ lb. skinless, boneless chicken thighs,
    cut into large bite-sized pieces
50 g/3½ tablespoons butter
1 large onion, finely chopped
1 cassia bark or cinnamon stick
4 cardamom pods
1 teaspoon mild or medium chilli/chili powder
1 x 400-g/14-oz. can chopped tomatoes
150 ml/⅔ cup chicken stock
100 ml/⅓ cup single/light cream
sea salt and freshly ground black pepper
fresh coriander/cilantro, chopped, to garnish

To serve

naan bread

SERVES 4

To make the marinade, heat a non-stick frying pan/skillet and toast the cashew nuts, fennel seeds, cinnamon, coriander, cardamom seeds, peppercorns and cloves for 2–3 minutes, or until very aromatic. Transfer to a spice grinder and grind until smooth.

Add this mixture to a blender with the garlic, ginger, vinegar, tomato purée and half the yogurt and process until smooth. Transfer to a large glass bowl with the remaining yogurt. Stir in the chicken, cover and refrigerate for 24 hours.

Melt the butter in a large, non-stick wok or saucepan and add the onion, cassia bark and cardamom pods. Stir-fry over a medium heat for 6–8 minutes, or until the onion has softened. Add the marinated chicken (discarding the marinade) and cook, stirring, for 10 minutes. Season. Stir in the chilli powder, canned tomatoes and stock, bring to a boil, then reduce the heat to low.

Simmer, uncovered, for 40–45 minutes, stirring occasionally. Add the cream and cook gently for a further 4–5 minutes.

Garnish with the coriander and serve immediately with naan bread.

1.5 kg/3 lb. 5 oz. chicken on the bone, portioned into pieces

For the marinade
2 tablespoons vegetable oil
½ lemon, freshly squeezed
2 tablespoons natural/plain yogurt
3 teaspoons Holy Trinity Paste
  (see page 29)
1 teaspoon Kashmiri chilli/chili powder
1½ teaspoons ground turmeric
1½ teaspoons ground cumin
1½ teaspoons ground coriander
1½ teaspoons sea salt
1 teaspoon garam masala

For the curry sauce
5 tablespoons vegetable oil
a 5-cm/2-inch cinnamon stick
5 cloves
2 star anise
3 fresh bay leaves
a 2.5-cm/1-inch squared piece
  of fresh ginger, grated
3 garlic cloves, crushed
2½ large onions, finely chopped
1 teaspoon sea salt
6 large tomatoes, chopped
  (core and seeds removed)
500 ml/2 cups water
1 teaspoon garam masala
2 tablespoons freshly chopped
  coriander/cilantro

To serve
boiled rice

SERVES 6

Perfect chicken curry

Not every curry sauce has to be rich and thick and this recipe proves it. The success of the dish lies in cooking the chicken on the bone, which not only keeps the meat moist, but also adds a depth of broth-like flavour to the sauce. The sauce itself is a relatively thin gravy which has different layers of flavour, created using a variety of spices at different stages of the cooking process.

Combine all of the ingredients for the marinade and mix together. Stir in the chicken and allow to marinate overnight in the fridge or for a minimum of 30 minutes at room temperature.

To make the curry sauce, heat the vegetable oil in a deep, heavy-based pan over a medium heat, add the cinnamon stick, cloves and star anise and fry for 1 minute to allow the aromatic oils of the spices to be released into the oil. Add the bay leaves, ginger and garlic and move around in the pan for 1 minute until the garlic and ginger are golden-brown. Add the onions and salt and fry until completely softened and golden-brown; about 25–30 minutes.

Add the tomatoes and cook until they have softened and melted and the ingredients are coming together to form a sauce base. Next, add the marinated chicken pieces, mixing really well in the pan and sealing them all over. Once sealed, pour in the water, mix well, place the lid on the pan and let the curry simmer for 20–25 minutes until the chicken is cooked and the liquid has reduced to give a sauce-like consistency. Add the garam masala and chopped coriander and serve with rice.

For the marinade

3 tablespoons vegetable oil
1 teaspoon Holy Trinity Paste (see page 29)
1 teaspoon sea salt
1 teaspoon ground cumin
1 teaspoon ground coriander
1 teaspoon paprika
1 teaspoon ground turmeric
2 tablespoons natural/plain yogurt
1 teaspoon tomato purée/paste
1 teaspoon garam masala

For the curry

1 kg/2¼ lb. chicken, diced
3 tablespoons ghee
a 5-cm/2-inch cinnamon or cassia bark stick
5 cloves
3 cardamom pods
1 teaspoon cumin seeds
3 onions, finely chopped
2 teaspoons sea salt
1 teaspoon Holy Trinity Paste (see page 29)
1 teaspoon ground cumin
1 teaspoon ground coriander
1 teaspoon ground turmeric
1 teaspoon paprika
2 tablespoons tomato purée/paste
2 large tomatoes, finely chopped
   (core and seeds removed)
450 ml/scant 2 cups water
a pinch of saffron strands
150 ml/⅔ cup double/heavy cream
100 ml/⅓ cup natural/plain yogurt
1 teaspoon dried fenugreek leaves
1 teaspoon garam masala

To serve

fresh coriander/cilantro, chopped
boiled rice

SERVES 6

Chicken saffron murgh mughali

Remember to start this rich and flavoursome recipe the day before.

Combine all of the ingredients for the marinade in a large mixing bowl, add the chicken and coat it well. Allow the chicken to marinate for 24 hours in the fridge. If you do not have time, you can marinate it for 30 minutes at room temperature.

Heat the ghee in a heavy-based pan over a medium heat and allow it to melt. Add the cinnamon stick, cloves and cardamom pods and fry for 1 minute. Add the cumin seeds and heat until they sizzle and pop.

Add the onions and salt and gently fry until soft and buttery; this will take a good 30 minutes, but be patient and allow the onions to really soften. Add a little more ghee or a splash of water if dry.

Add the Holy Trinity Paste, mix and fry for 2–3 minutes. Add the ground spices and a splash more water and fry for 4–5 minutes. Add the tomato purée, mix well and fry for 2–3 minutes. Now add the tomatoes, mix in well, cover and cook over a low heat for 20 minutes. Add the marinated chicken and mix really well so that the chicken is well coated with the sauce. Once the chicken is sealed, add the water and simmer gently for around 25–30 minutes. Next, add the saffron strands, cream and yogurt, mix really well and simmer for a further 5 minutes. Add the fenugreek leaves and garam masala, then stir.

Sprinkle with fresh coriander and serve with rice.

Indian pepper chicken

This curry is laced with spicy and aromatic crushed Malabar peppercorns from India's south-west coast. Dried fruit adds a touch of sweetness to the dish.

For the pickled carrots & raisins

6 carrots, grated
100 g/¾ cup raisins
2 shallots, thinly sliced
1 teaspoon Lampong peppercorns chopped
1 quantity of Basic Pickle Mix (see below)
½ teaspoon ground cumin
½ teaspoon ground coriander

For the basic pickle mix

475 ml/2 cups white wine vinegar
100 g/½ cup caster/white granulated sugar
1 teaspoon sea salt
1 bay leaf

For the chicken

8 chicken thighs, skin on, bone in
2 teaspoons ground Malabar pepper
1 teaspoon sea salt
4 tablespoons ghee or olive oil
1 onion, diced
2 garlic cloves, crushed
1 teaspoon curry powder
1 teaspoon ground turmeric
1 teaspoon ancho chilli/chili powder
1 teaspoon ground cumin
4 sprigs of fresh curry leaves
475 ml/2 cups chicken stock
70 g/½ cup raisins or dried dates

To serve

naan bread

a sterilized screw-top jar

SERVES 4

The pickled carrots and raisins need to be made at least 1 week in advance to allow the flavours to infuse. Layer the carrot, raisins, shallots and peppercorns in a sterilized jar. Bring the Basic Pickle Mix to a boil, then add the cumin and coriander, and stir to dissolve the sugar. Cook for 3 minutes, then pour into the jar and screw the lid on. To seal, screw the lid on the jar while still warm, turn it upside down to cool completely, then put in the fridge for at least 1 week before eating or storing in the cupboard. Once opened, consume within 6 months.

Sprinkle the chicken thighs with the pepper and salt, making sure they are completely coated. Set a large frying pan/skillet over a medium–high heat and add 3 tablespoons of the ghee or oil. Put the chicken skin side down in the pan and sauté for about 4 minutes, until golden brown. Turn the chicken over and brown the other side, then transfer over to a large plate.

Add the remaining ghee or oil to the pan, and add the onion and garlic and cook until golden brown (about 5 minutes). Add the curry powder, turmeric, chilli powder and cumin, and stir to combine. Cook for 2 minutes.

Return the chicken to the pan, skin side down, and top with the curry leaves. Pour over the chicken stock and bring to a boil, then reduce the heat to a simmer and cover the pan with a lid or foil. Cook for 30 minutes. Remove the lid and toss in the raisins or dates. Turn the chicken thighs over and continue to cook uncovered for another 30 minutes.

Serve the chicken with the sauce, warm naan bread and pickled carrots and raisins.

Jerk chicken

There's chicken, and then there's marinated, grilled, perfectly spiced, finger-lickin' chicken. This is that kind of chicken, and it goes perfectly with mac 'n' cheese (see page 46).

1 tablespoon ground allspice
1 teaspoon dried thyme
1½ teaspoons cayenne pepper
1½ teaspoons ground black pepper
1½ teaspoons dried sage
¾ teaspoon ground nutmeg
¾ teaspoon ground cinnamon
1 tablespoon caster/white granulated sugar
4 tablespoons olive oil
4 tablespoons soy sauce
175 ml/¾ cup white vinegar
125 ml/½ cup orange juice
juice of 1 lime, freshly squeezed
1 Habanero or Scotch Bonnet chilli/chile, deseeded and finely chopped
3 spring onions/scallions, finely chopped
1 onion, finely chopped
10 garlic cloves, crushed
4–6 chicken breasts, or a whole chicken cut into pieces (skin left on)

a charcoal grill/broiler or barbecue

SERVES 4

Combine the first 8 ingredients in a large bowl.

Combine the olive oil, soy sauce, vinegar, orange juice and lime juice in a large measuring cup or small bowl. Slowly add the spice mixture, whisking it in until incorporated. Add the chilli pepper, spring onions, onion and garlic and stir to finish the marinade.

Spread the marinade all over the chicken pieces. Place in a large resealable plastic bag and seal tightly Marinate in the fridge overnight, or for at least 4 hours.

When ready to cook, heat up either a barbecue or a charcoal grill/broiler.

Grill/broil the chicken for about 6 minutes per side, brushing on more of the marinade while cooking and making sure that the marinade is well cooked (it will have been in contact with the raw chicken for several hours). Test if the chicken is cooked through by sticking a skewer in the thickest part – if the juices run clear, it is ready. Bring the leftover marinade to a fast boil for at least 4 minutes and serve as a dipping sauce.

Serve on its own, or with mac 'n' cheese (see page 46).

Chicken fajitas *with mild guacamole*

This is a very popular and sociable meal. Simply lay all of the elements out on the table and let people help themselves.

800 g/1¾ lb. skinless, boneless chicken
    breasts, cut into strips
2 orange (bell) peppers, deseeded and sliced
2 courgettes/zucchini, sliced
2 onions, halved and sliced
1 x 28-g/1-oz. pack fajita seasoning
4 tablespoons olive oil
8 tortilla wraps or lettuce leaves

For the guacamole
2 ripe avocados, peeled and stoned/pitted
5 g/¼ cup fresh coriander/cilantro,
    stems and leaves
70 g/2½ oz. red onion, finely diced
½ tablespoon lime juice, freshly squeezed
1 plum tomato, peeled and deseeded
4 tablespoons extra virgin olive oil
sea salt and freshly ground black pepper

To serve
lime wedges, for squeezing

SERVES 4

Preheat the oven to 220°C (425°F) Gas 7.

In a large bowl, mix together the chicken strips, peppers, courgettes and onions. In a separate bowl, mix the fajita seasoning and olive oil, then combine the seasoning/oil mix with the chicken mix and stir to make sure everything is coated evenly. When thoroughly coated, spread this mix out on a large sheet pan.

Bake in the preheated oven for 15 minutes or until the chicken is cooked through and the vegetables are soft, stirring once.

Meanwhile, make the guacamole. Put all the guacamole ingredients into a food processor and blend to a chunky paste.

Finally, just before you remove the chicken and vegetables from the oven, warm the tortillas or prepare the lettuce leaves.

Serve the fajita chicken and vegetables with the guacamole and the wraps/lettuce leaves, and lime wedges for squeezing over.

Red hot buffalo wings

Frank's Red Hot Buffalo Sauce was the 'secret' ingredient used to create the original Buffalo-style wings in Buffalo, New York. It's essentially hot sauce made with cayenne pepper. This recipe has a hot base, but the use of butter gives it a slightly milder flavour.

canola or peanut oil, for frying

1.8 kg/4 lb. chicken wings, halved at the joints, tips removed

170 g/1 stick plus 4 tablespoons butter

250 ml/1 cup Frank's Red Hot Buffalo hot sauce or other hot sauce

For the blue cheese dip

150 g/1 cup crumbled blue cheese

150 g/¾ cup mayonnaise

120 ml/½ cup sour cream

To serve

carrot sticks

celery sticks

a deep fryer

SERVES 4–6

Make the Blue Cheese Dip first. Place all the ingredients in a medium bowl and whisk until combined.

Preheat the oven to 100°C (200°F) Gas ¼.

Preheat the oil in a deep fryer set to 180°C (350°F).

Dry the wings thoroughly with paper towels/kitchen paper. Working in batches, fry the wings for about 12 minutes until golden brown and the juices run clear when the thickest part is pierced to the bone. Transfer the cooked wings to a wire rack set over a baking sheet, and place in the oven to keep warm until all the wings have been fried.

Heat the butter in a 30-cm/12-inch deep-sided frying pan/skillet over a medium heat. Stir in the hot sauce until smooth, then add the wings, and toss until completely coated. Serve the wings in a large bowl with Blue Cheese Dip and celery and carrot sticks on the side.

Damn hot wings

These are the hottest chicken wings in the whole book. A variety of hot chillies/chiles are used, along with a spicy hot sauce. These are not for the faint of heart!

vegetable oil or canola oil, for frying
1.8 kg/4 lb. chicken wings, halved
    at the joints, tips removed
115 g/1 stick butter
750 ml/3 cups hot sauce
2 tablespoons garlic cloves, crushed
3 jalapeño chillies/chiles, deseeded and sliced
2 Thai chillies/chiles, deseeded and sliced
3 Habanero chillies/chiles, deseeded and sliced
2 yellow wax peppers, deseeded and sliced
3 red chillies/chiles, deseeded and sliced
sea salt and freshly ground black pepper

a deep fryer

SERVES 4–6

Preheat the oil in a deep fryer set to 180°C (350°F). Preheat the oven to 200°C (400°F) Gas 6.

Fry the wings, 3–4 at a time, turning occasionally, until golden brown. Transfer to a shallow baking dish and bake in the preheated oven for 15 minutes, turning once, or until the juices run clear when the thickest part is pierced to the bone.

Melt the butter in a medium saucepan over a medium heat. Stir in the hot sauce, garlic and peppers. Reduce the heat to medium-low and cook for 15 minutes, or until the peppers have softened. Season to taste with salt and pepper, then pour the sauce over the wings, turning to coat.

Reduce the oven temperature to 180°C (350°F) Gas 4, return the wings to the oven and bake for a further 10 minutes.

These wings are great served with Blue Cheese Dip (see page 93).

Spicy Thai-style fried wings

America has been on a fried chicken craze for a fair few years now. And let's be honest, fried chicken isn't so much a craze as it is a way of life. This recipe is spicy, crispy and perfect for anything from picnics to family parties and get-togethers.

For the lemongrass & soy dipping sauce

3 stalks of lemongrass

2 spring onions/scallions, chopped

1 teaspoon finely chopped garlic

1 teaspoon brown sugar

1 tablespoon sriracha sauce

3 tablespoons lime juice, freshly squeezed

1 tablespoon fish sauce

2 teaspoons soy sauce

1 tablespoon freshly chopped coriander/cilantro

1 tablespoon freshly chopped basil

3 tablespoons water

For the wings

1.8 kg/4 lbs. chicken wings,
    halved at the joints, tips removed

9 garlic cloves

7.5-cm/3-in. piece of fresh ginger, grated

6 tablespoons soy sauce

6 tablespoons curry paste

3 tablespoons rice vinegar

2 tablespoons coconut oil, melted

2 tablespoons runny honey

180 g/1⅓ cups plain/all-purpose flour

2 tablespoons cornflour/cornstarch

350 ml/1⅔ cups water

vegetable or canola oil, for frying

a deep fryer

SERVES 4–6

First, make the Lemongrass & Soy Dipping Sauce. Trim the end of the lemongrass stalks and remove the outer layers, then finely chop. Place in a bowl with he other ingredients. Mix well, then chill in the fridge.

Preheat the oil in a deep fryer to 180°C (350°F).

Chop the garlic and ginger by pulsing briefly in a food processor. Add the soy sauce, curry paste, vinegar, coconut oil and honey. Purée until smooth. Put the sauce into a bowl.

In a separate bowl, whisk the flour and cornflour with the water. Add the chicken and toss until well coated. Fry the chicken in about 3 batches for 6–8 minutes until golden, then drain on paper towels/kitchen paper.

Bring the oil back to 180°C (350°F) and fry the chicken for a further 6–8 minutes, until crisp and the juices run clear when the thickest part is pierced to the bone. Drain again, then toss the chicken in the sauce. Serve with the Lemongrass & Soy Dipping Sauce.

Coconut curry wings

These chicken wings are fried and then tossed in a flavoursome coconut-curry sauce. This dish goes perfectly with rice or naan bread.

For the marinade
85 g/½ cup coconut oil
4 teaspoons Jamaican/Caribbean curry powder
4 teaspoons garlic powder
1 teaspoon ground ginger
a pinch of sea salt
a pinch of freshly ground black pepper

For the coconut curry sauce
2 tablespoons coconut oil
1 garlic clove, crushed
2 tablespoons freshly grated ginger
2 tablespoons Jamaican/Caribbean
    curry powder
1 teaspoon crushed chilli/hot red pepper flakes
400 ml/1¾ cups coconut milk
3 tablespoons runny honey
2 tablespoons soy sauce
juice of 2 limes, freshly squeezed,
    plus a squeeze for serving
a couple of pinches of nutmeg

For the wings
1.8 kg/4 lb. chicken wings, halved
    at the joints, tips removed
vegetable oil, for frying

To serve
1 cucumber, and 3 radishes, chopped
    into chunks
a handful of fresh coriander/cilantro, chopped

2–3 baking sheets, lined with foil
a deep fryer

SERVES 4–6

Combine the coconut oil, curry powder, garlic, ginger, salt and pepper together in a small saucepan and heat gently until the coconut oil has melted. Slather on the wings and place in a large resealable plastic bag. Place in the fridge and marinate for at least 4 hours.

Prepare the Coconut Curry Sauce. Combine the coconut oil with the garlic, ginger, curry powder and chilli flakes in a medium saucepan and cook gently for 2 minutes. Add the coconut milk, honey, soy sauce, lime juice and nutmeg. Bring to a light simmer and let reduce for 40–45 minutes until it reaches a thicker consistency. Keep warm whilst you prepare the wings.

Preheat the oil in a deep fryer set to 180°C (350°F).

Preheat the oven to 200°C (400°F) Gas 6.

Fry the wings, a few at a time, for 6–8 minutes until they are golden brown. Place the fried wings on the prepared baking sheets and bake in the preheated oven for 5 minutes for extra crispness or until the juices run clear when the thickest part is pierced to the bone.

Once the wings are done, toss with sauce in a large mixing bowl. Garnish with the cucumber and radish chunks and a squeeze of lime before serving.

Yakitori-glazed chicken
& mushroom skewers

These salty-sweet glazed chicken skewers go down well with all the family! Fresh shiitake mushrooms, with their distinctive flavour, are a pleasing element in the dish. Serve simply with jasmine rice or sushi rice and blanched pak choi/bok choy, gai laan or spinach.

16 white/cup mushrooms, stalks trimmed off

250 g/8 oz. skinless, boneless chicken breast, cut into short, thin strips

16 fresh shiitake mushrooms, halved, stalks trimmed off

½ green (bell) pepper, deseeded and cut into 2-cm/¾-inch squares

2 spring onions/scallions, cut into 2-cm/¾-inch lengths

finely chopped red chilli/chile, to garnish (optional)

For the yakitori glaze

3 tablespoons rice wine or Amontillado sherry

3 tablespoons mirin

3 tablespoons light soy sauce

1 tablespoon caster/white granulated sugar

¼ teaspoon sea salt

8 metal or soaked wooden cooking skewers

SERVES 4

Make the yakitori glaze by placing the rice wine or sherry, mirin, soy sauce, sugar and salt in a small saucepan. Bring to a boil and boil for 1 minute until melted together into a syrupy glaze. Turn off the heat.

Thread the white mushrooms, chicken, shiitake mushrooms, green pepper and spring onions onto the 8 skewers.

Preheat the grill/broiler. Brush the skewers generously with the yakitori glaze. Grill/broil the skewers for 8–10 minutes until the chicken is cooked through, brushing repeatedly with the glaze and turning over the skewers halfway through. Serve at once.

Mango & chilli-marinated chicken

In this recipe you cook the chicken in the marinade, turning it into something of a cook-in sauce. This works well with homemade marinades as they tend not to have the acidity (needed to extend shelf life) of store-bought versions.

1 teaspoon mixed peppercorns
1 teaspoon coriander/cilantro seeds
½ teaspoon cumin seeds
1 teaspoon fenugreek seeds
½ teaspoon fennel seeds
1 teaspoon sea salt
200 g/6½ oz. fresh mango flesh, diced (from 1 mango, about 300 g/10 oz.)
4 tablespoons white wine vinegar
4 teaspoons caster/white granulated sugar
1 small Habanero or other very hot chilli/chile, deseeded and very finely chopped
2 garlic cloves, crushed
a handful of fresh coriander/cilantro, chopped
1–2 tablespoons olive oil, if required
4 large skinless, boneless chicken breasts

To serve
cooked pilaf rice
plain/natural yogurt

a deep ovenproof dish

SERVES 4

Toast the spices in a hot, dry frying pan/skillet over a medium heat until the seeds start to pop. Grind them, together with the salt, using a pestle and mortar. Put the ground spices, mango, vinegar, sugar, chilli, garlic and coriander into a food processor and blend for about 30 seconds, or until smooth. If required, loosen the marinade with 1–2 tablespoons olive oil.

Lightly score the chicken breasts with a sharp knife, place them into a deep bowl and cover with the marinade. Use your hands to rub the marinade well into the meat. Cover and refrigerate for at least 2 hours. This can be done in the morning and left to marinate until evening.

Preheat the oven to 180°C (350°F) Gas 4.

Place the chicken and its marinade in the deep ovenproof dish, cover with foil and cook in the preheated oven for 30 minutes. Remove the foil and return the chicken to the oven for a further 10 minutes, or until it is cooked through and the juices run clear.

Serve on a bed of pilaf rice with a dollop of yogurt

Peruvian-style chilli & garlic chicken with new potatoes

This chicken dish is incredibly flavoursome and is great to warm up cold winter evenings.

800 g–1 kg/1¾–2¼ lb. small/medium waxy new potatoes, washed and cut into even sizes
25 g/2 tablespoons butter
6 large skinless, boneless chicken breasts
2 slices of lemon
2 fresh bay leaves
200 ml/¾ cup vegetable or chicken stock
120 ml/½ cup sunflower oil
3 onions, chopped
6 garlic cloves, crushed
4 Rocoto chillies/chiles, deseeded and finely chopped
450 g/1 lb. (about 3 cups) roasted unsalted peanuts, roughly chopped
½ teaspoon ground cinnamon
120 g/1½ cups finely grated hard cheese, eg Parmesan cheese
1 tablespoon cumin seeds, crushed
180 ml/¾ cup plain/natural yogurt, at room temperature, plus extra to serve
sea salt and freshly ground black pepper

To serve
wilted spinach

SERVES 6

Boil the potatoes in a pan of lightly salted water for 15–20 minutes until they are nearly cooked but still a little firm. Drain and set aside in the pan with the lid on.

Meanwhile, heat the butter in a wok-style frying pan/skillet or sauté pan over a medium heat. Gently fry the chicken breasts until they are sealed and slightly browned. Add the lemon slices, bay leaves and stock and season with salt and pepper. Cover and bring to a simmer. Cook for about 20 minutes, or until the chicken is just cooked but still moist.

Remove the pan from the heat. Lift the chicken out of the pan, wrap in foil to retain moistness and set aside. Leaving the stock in the pan, return to the heat. Add the nearly cooked new potatoes, turn the heat up to medium/high and continue to cook, uncovered, for about 15 minutes, tossing frequently until the remaining liquid has evaporated from the pan. Remove the pan from the heat, fish out the bay leaves and discard. There is no need to remove the lemon slices as they will have softened and will taste delicious. Cover the pan and set aside.

Heat the oil in a large saucepan. Add the onions and garlic and cook gently over a very low heat for about 5 minutes, or until softened. Add the chillies, peanuts, cinnamon, cheese and cumin and mix together. Cook for 5 minutes.

Meanwhile, unwrap the cooked chicken and tear into generous strips. Add to the peanut mixture, stir in the yogurt and season with salt and pepper. Gently heat through. Serve with the deliciously flavoured sautéed potatoes, extra yogurt and maybe some simple wilted spinach.

Cajun fried chicken

Fried chicken is a real summer dish especially suited to those long sunny days spent at the beach. Wrap it up for a picnic as it's as delicious eaten cold as hot. Generously sprinkle with lemon zest and sea salt for that extra tang and serve with an array of hot sauces.

For the cajun seasoning
2 teaspoons cumin
2 teaspoons cayenne
2 tablespoons Spanish smoked paprika
2 teaspoons dried oregano
1 teaspoon dried garlic powder
1 teaspoon sea salt
1 teaspoon freshly ground black pepper

For the fried chicken
2–kg/4–lb. chicken, cut into 10 pieces
375 ml/1½ cups buttermilk
1 egg
130 g/1 cup plain/all-purpose flour
75 g/½ cup polenta/cornmeal
1.4 litres/6 cups vegetable oil, for frying
sea salt, for sprinkling
lemon zest, for sprinkling
lemon wedges, for squeezing

a deep fryer

SERVES 4–6

To make the Cajun seasoning, mix all the ingredients together in a small bowl.

Place the chicken pieces in a large ceramic baking dish. In a bowl whisk together the buttermilk, egg, and 2 tablespoons of the Cajun seasoning. Pour over the chicken, making sure the pieces are evenly coated. Cover and refrigerate for 4–24 hours.

In a shallow bowl mix together the flour, polenta, and 1 tablespoon of the Cajun seasoning. (Store the remaining seasoning in an airtight container.)

Remove the chicken from the fridge and bring to room temperature. Pour the oil into a 5-quart/5-litre saucepan/Dutch oven or deep fryer and heat to 375°F/190°C. Remove the chicken from the buttermilk and shake off any excess marinade. Dredge each piece in the flour mix and, working in batches, fry the chicken in the hot oil for 8–10 minutes. Cook until dark golden brown and cooked all the way through.

Remove the chicken pieces from the oil, drain on paper towels/kitchen paper, and sprinkle with the sea salt and lemon zest. Serve with lemon wedges and store-bought hot sauces, if you like.

Chicken mole burrito

A mole is a deliciously spicy Mexican sauce. In this recipe, it is made from ready-made mole paste because it can be labour-intensive to make and difficult to source the ingredients.

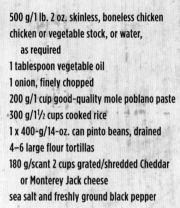

500 g/1 lb. 2 oz. skinless, boneless chicken
chicken or vegetable stock, or water,
   as required
1 tablespoon vegetable oil
1 onion, finely chopped
200 g/1 cup good-quality mole poblano paste
300 g/1½ cups cooked rice
1 x 400-g/14-oz. can pinto beans, drained
4–6 large flour tortillas
180 g/scant 2 cups grated/shredded Cheddar
   or Monterey Jack cheese
sea salt and freshly ground black pepper

SERVES 4–6

Put the chicken in a large saucepan and add enough stock or water to cover. If using water or unseasoned stock, season with salt.

Bring to a boil over a medium heat, then cover and simmer gently for 30–40 minutes until cooked through and tender. Remove the chicken from the pan and let cool slightly, then shred using your hands or 2 forks. Taste and adjust the seasoning.

Preheat the oven to 200°C (400°F) Gas 6.

Heat the oil in a saucepan set over a medium-high heat. Add the onion and cook for about 5–8 minutes, stirring occasionally, until golden. Stir in the mole paste and dilute according to the package instructions, using a little stock or water. Cook for 1–2 minutes further. Add the shredded chicken, rice and beans and mix well. Simmer over a low heat for 10–15 minutes.

Divide the chicken mixture between the tortillas and sprinkle with grated cheese. Fold in the sides of each tortilla to cover the filling, then roll up to enclose. Place the filled tortillas seam-side down on a greased baking sheet or in a shallow dish. Cover with foil and bake in the preheated oven for 10–15 minutes just to warm through and melt the cheese. Serve hot.

Spanish-style chicken & rice

This is really a cheat's paella, but it tastes just as good as the real thing. The shortcut here is the oven baking; easier than stirring and watching over the stovetop like a hawk. It's a meal in itself, but a nice bottle of Spanish red and some crusty bread would not go amiss.

1 tablespoon olive oil
8 chicken thighs, trimmed of excess skin
 and fat
1 onion, diced
1 orange or yellow (bell) pepper, deseeded
 and diced
1 carrot, diced
4 garlic cloves, crushed
½ teaspoon Spanish smoked sweet paprika
380 g/2 cups paella rice
6–8 cooking chorizo (about 250 g/9 oz.),
 cut into large pieces
125 ml/½ cup plus 1 teaspoon dry white wine
300 ml/1¼ cups plus 1 teaspoon chicken stock
1 x 400-g/14-oz. can chopped tomatoes
1 bay leaf
200 g/1½ cups frozen peas
a large handful of fresh flat-leaf
 parsley, chopped
sea salt and freshly ground black pepper

a large flameproof casserole dish/Dutch oven

SERVES 4

Preheat the oven to 200°C (400°F) Gas 6.

Heat the oil in a casserole dish. Add the chicken, skin-side down, and cook for 3–5 minutes on each side, until browned. Transfer to a plate and season with salt.

Add the onion, pepper and carrot to the casserole dish and cook for 2–3 minutes. Add the garlic, paprika, rice and chorizo and continue cooking, stirring to coat the rice in oil, for about 1 minute more.

Stir in the wine, stock and tomatoes, add the bay leaf and season well. Return the chicken to the casserole. Cover with a lid and transfer to the preheated oven. Cook for 20 minutes. Remove the casserole from the oven and stir in the peas. Return to the oven and cook for a further 10 minutes, until the rice is tender. If it seems dry when adding the peas, add a splash of water.

Remove from the oven and let stand, covered, for about 10 minutes. Remove the bay leaf, stir in the parsley, fluff up the rice with a fork and serve.

Chicken pot pie

This version of a classic dish is designed to be quick comfort food, so if the crème fraîche doesn't appeal, replace with a white sauce or whatever you prefer.

55 g/4 tablespoons butter
1 leek, trimmed and sliced
2 carrots, sliced
450 g/1 lb. skinless, boneless chicken breast, cubed
8 leaves of fresh tarragon, chopped
3 tablespoons freshly chopped flat-leaf parsley
150 g/generous 1 cup fresh or frozen peas
250 ml/1 cup crème fraîche or double/ heavy cream
500g/1 lb store-bought puff pastry
2 egg yolks, lightly beaten with a pinch of sea salt, to glaze
sea salt and freshly ground black pepper

a 1-litre/4-cup ovenproof dish

SERVES 4

Melt the butter in a medium saucepan and add the leek and carrots. Cook for about 10 minutes or until they are both soft and cooked through. Add the chicken, stir well and cook for about 10 minutes until the chicken is cooked through. Stir in the tarragon and parsley, followed by the peas and crème fraîche. Bring to a boil, then remove from the heat and set aside.

Roll out the pastry on a lightly floured surface and cut it at least 2.5 cm/1 inch wider than the top of your ovenproof dish.

Spoon the chicken filling evenly into the dish, brush the edges of the dish with a little beaten egg yolk and top with pastry. Press the pastry firmly down onto the edges of the dish to seal. You may like to crimp or fork the edges. (There's need for a hole in the lid – the puff pastry wants to rise up into a dome.) Brush with beaten egg yolk and chill for at least 30 minutes.

Preheat the oven to 200°C (400°F) Gas 6.

Remove the pie from the fridge, brush with more beaten egg yolk (thinned down with a little water or milk if necessary) to build up a nice glaze, then set the dish on a large baking sheet. Bake in the preheated oven for about 30 minutes or until the pastry top is puffed and golden and the pie is bubbling hot inside. Serve hot.

Roast chicken *with broad beans & lemon*

This is a perfect relaxed, easy summer Sunday roast. It's tasty, colourful and earthy.

375 g/2½ cups fresh shelled broad/
   fava beans
2 tablespoons olive oil
1.5 kg/3¼ lb. chicken pieces, bone in,
   skin on
3 onions, roughly chopped
a handful of fresh thyme
zest and juice of 2 unwaxed lemons,
   freshly grated and squeezed
3 garlic cloves, thinly sliced
350 ml/1½ cups fresh chicken stock
a handful of fresh mint leaves
2 tablespoons capers, rinsed
sea salt and freshly ground black pepper

a casserole dish/Dutch oven

SERVES 4

Preheat the oven to 200°C (400°F) Gas 6.

Bring a pan of water to the boil. Add the broad beans and boil for 2 minutes. Drain and refresh under cold running water. Peel away the skins and discard. Set aside.

Heat the oil in a large flameproof casserole dish/ Dutch oven over a high heat. Cook the chicken pieces in 2 batches, for 4 minutes on each side until browned. Remove from the dish and set aside.

Add the onions, thyme and lemon zest to the casserole dish and cook for 2 minutes. Return the chicken and any juices to the dish with the garlic and stock. Bring to a boil, and add salt and pepper.

Transfer to the preheated oven and cook uncovered for 40 minutes.

Stir in the broad beans, 2 tablespoons of lemon juice and top with mint and capers. Season with salt and pepper to taste and serve.

Sautéed chicken with white wine, pea & tarragon sauce

This is one of the easiest supper dishes imaginable. It takes less time to cook than a ready meal and it is much more delicious.

1 tablespoon olive oil

100 g/3½ oz. pancetta cubes or dry-cured streaky/fatty bacon, chopped

2 skinless, boneless chicken breasts, cut into thin slices

1 onion, very finely chopped

125 ml/½ cup dry white wine

150 g/1 cup fresh podded or frozen peas

2 tablespoons freshly chopped tarragon leaves

100 g/4 rounded tablespoons crème fraiche/ sour cream

freshly ground black pepper

To serve

steamed asparagus tips

SERVES 2

Heat the oil in a large frying pan/ skillet, then add the pancetta cubes or bacon. Fry for a couple of minutes until the fat starts to run. Add the chicken slices and fry, stirring occasionally, until lightly golden, around 4–5 minutes.

Add the onion to the pan and fry for 1–2 minutes. Add the wine and peas and cook until the wine has reduced by about two-thirds. Reduce the heat and stir in the tarragon, crème fraiche and black pepper, to taste. Heat gently until almost bubbling.

Remove the pan from the heat. Transfer the sautéed chicken to 2 warm plates, spoon over the sauce and serve with steamed asparagus tips.

Chicken cacciatore

Chicken cacciatore translates as 'hunter's chicken'. Classic Italian ingredients, including tomatoes, garlic and wine, are transformed into a thick, tasty sauce that coats the chicken.

600 g/1¼ lb. ripe tomatoes
4 chicken drumsticks
4 chicken thighs
plain/all-purpose flour, to coat
3 tablespoons olive oil
1 slice pancetta, diced
2 garlic cloves, crushed
4 sprigs of rosemary
1 yellow (bell) pepper, deseeded and sliced
75 ml/⅓ cup dry white wine
1 tablespoon tomato purée/paste
sea salt and freshly ground black pepper

a casserole dish/Dutch oven

SERVES 4

Begin by scalding the tomatoes. Pour boiling water over the ripe tomatoes in a heatproof bowl. Set aside for 1 minute, then drain and carefully peel off the skins using a sharp knife. Roughly chop, reserving any juices, and set aside.

Season the chicken pieces with salt and pepper, then season the flour with salt and pepper in a wide, shallow dish. Coat the chicken pieces in the seasoned flour, ready to fry.

In a large frying pan/skillet, heat 2 tablespoons of the oil. Fry the chicken in batches, until golden-brown on all sides.

Heat the remaining oil in a casserole dish. Add the pancetta and garlic and fry, stirring occasionally, for 1–2 minutes, until the garlic is lightly browned. Add the rosemary and the pepper and fry for 1 minute. Pour in the wine and cook, stirring occasionally, for 1–2 minutes, until the wine has reduced slightly. Add the chopped tomatoes with their juices, cover and cook for 5 minutes, until the sauce has come to a boil. Stir well, to help the tomatoes break down, then stir in the tomato purée. Season with salt and pepper and simmer uncovered for 10 minutes, stirring occasionally.

Add the browned chicken pieces to the tomato sauce. Bring to a boil, reduce the heat and simmer, partly covered, for 20–30 minutes, until the chicken is cooked through.

Chicken with white wine & chanterelles

This dish is perfect for a romantic dinner for two. You need only a glass of wine for cooking the chicken, so the rest of the bottle can be enjoyed with the meal.

15 g/⅓ cup dried chanterelles

1 tablespoon plain/all-purpose flour

2 boneless chicken breasts, skin on

2 tablespoons olive oil

35 g/2 tablespoons plus
   1 teaspoon butter

4 shallots, thinly sliced

a pinch of Spanish sweet
   smoked paprika

150 ml/⅔ cup good-quality
   white wine

3 tablespoons double/heavy cream

2 coils dried pappardelle all'uovo or
   other wide-ribboned egg pasta,
   about 100 g/3½ oz.

freshly grated nutmeg

1 tablespoon freshly chopped
   flat-leaf parsley

sea salt and freshly ground
   black pepper

an ovenproof dish

SERVES 2

Soak the chanterelles in water for 15 minutes. Drain the chanterelles, reserve the soaking liquid and strain it through a fine sieve/strainer.

Preheat the oven to 200°C (400°F) Gas 6.

Put the flour in a shallow dish and season it with salt and pepper. Dip the chicken breasts into the flour and coat both sides. Heat a medium frying pan/skillet over a moderate heat, add 1 tablespoon olive oil and 10 g/2 teaspoons butter. When the butter is foaming, add the chicken breasts skin-side down. Fry for 2½–3 minutes until the skin is brown and crisp. Turn the chicken over and lightly brown the other side for 2½–3 minutes.

Transfer the chicken to an ovenproof dish and cook in the preheated oven for 15–20 minutes until cooked.

Meanwhile, discard the fat from the frying pan/skillet and wipe the pan with paper towels/kitchen paper. Heat the remaining oil and 15 g/1 tablespoon butter in the pan, add the shallots and fry gently for 5–6 minutes or until soft. Stir in the paprika, then increase the heat to high and add the wine. When the wine has reduced by half, add 90 ml/⅓ cup of the reserved mushroom water. Reduce the heat and let simmer gently for 10 minutes. Strain the sauce through a fine sieve/strainer into a heatproof bowl.

Return the strained sauce to the pan, add the chanterelles, cover and simmer for 10 minutes. Remove the pan from the heat, stir in the cream and salt and pepper to taste. Return the pan to the burner and heat very gently, stirring occasionally, until the sauce thickens up.

To cook the pasta, bring a large saucepan of lightly salted water to a boil, add the pasta and cook until al dente. Drain well, add the remaining butter and season with pepper and freshly grated nutmeg. Cut each chicken breast into thick diagonal slices.

Divide the pasta between 2 plates, and top with the chicken, mushrooms and cream. Scatter over the parsley and serve hot.

Coq au vin

This recipe still takes a little time in the oven but it's a simpler approach than the traditional.

For the white chicken stock

1.5 litres/6¼ cups water
1 onion, chopped
2 garlic cloves (optional), chopped
1 carrot, chopped
2 celery sticks, chopped
1 bay leaf
a pinch of freshly ground
    black pepper
1 teaspoon whole pink peppercorns
carcass of 1 whole chicken

MAKES ABOUT 150 ML/⅔ CUP

1 whole jointed chicken
250 ml/1 cup red wine
3 bay leaves
2 garlic cloves, chopped
3 tablespoons olive oil
45 g/3 tablespoons butter
75 g/generous 1 cup chopped
    mushrooms
6 shallots, chopped
85 g/3 oz. pancetta, diced
2 tablespoons plain/all-purpose flour
400 ml/1⅔ cups White Chicken Stock
juice of ½ lemon, freshly squeezed
sea salt and freshly ground
    black pepper

To serve

steamed green beans (optional)
cooked rice (optional)

a casserole dish/Dutch oven

SERVES 4

Prepare the white chicken stock in advance. Bring the water to a boil in a pan with a lid. Then add the vegetables, bay leaf, black pepper and peppercorns and return to boil. Add the chicken carcass and then reduce the heat to a simmer and leave to cook over a low heat, covered, for 3 hours. Occasionally, skim the surface – you can just use a sieve/strainer or some paper towels/kitchen paper to run over the top of the water. After 3 hours, strain the liquid into a bowl and allow to cool. Once it's at room temperature, transfer it to the fridge. Keep chilled for up to 8 days.

To make the Coq Au Vin, you will need to keep the thighs and drumsticks on the bone but debone the breast joint and cut it into smaller thirds. Put the chicken in a bowl with the red wine, bay leaves, garlic and 1 tablespoon of the olive oil. Cover the bowl and leave in the fridge to marinate for at least 1 hour, or overnight.

Preheat the oven to 160°C (325°F) Gas 3. Heat half the butter in a large, deep frying pan/skillet and add the pancetta, shallots and mushrooms, season with salt and papper and fry over a high heat for 5 minutes, until the pancetta browns. Take the chicken out of the bowl, leaving the marinade in there for the moment, and add the chicken to the mushrooms, shallots and pancetta for a few minutes, until sealed. Add the marinade from the bowl and stir. Sprinkle the flour over the top and leave undisturbed for a minute to absorb flavours, then stir in.

Add the stock and lemon juice. Mix well and then transfer the contents to a casserole dish/Dutch oven. Cover with a lid (or with foil) and cook in the preheated oven for 1½ hours. If you want to remove the bones, remove the thighs and drumsticks and carefully pinch them to remove the bones – make sure you find the fibula bone on both drumsticks (the very thin, needle-like bone). Return the meat to the casserole and use a fork to break the tender chicken chunks into shreds. Mix together. Alternatively, leave the meat on the bone and serve in whole pieces. Serve with green beans or with rice for a fuller meal.

Spanish-style red pepper & chicken bake

This is a dish that tastes of Spanish getaways. It cooks whilst you plan your next summer vacation.

8–10 new potatoes, cut into quarters, lengthways
1 teaspoon olive oil
1 teaspoon sea salt
1 onion, finely chopped
1 garlic clove, crushed
1 red (bell) pepper, deseeded and finely chopped
½ teaspoon dried marjoram or oregano
¾ teaspoon smoked paprika
1 x 400-g/14-oz. can chopped tomatoes
200 g/7 oz. mini chicken fillets
1 tablespoon freshly chopped oregano

SERVES 2

Preheat the oven to 200°C (400°F) Gas 6.

Put the potatoes on a small sheet pan with sides, drizzle over the olive oil and sprinkle over ¼ teaspoon salt.

Bake in the preheated oven for 20 minutes. Make sure the potatoes are almost cooked. If not, you can give them a little longer in the oven.

Meanwhile, make the sauce. Combine the onion, garlic, red pepper, herbs, paprika, the remaining salt and tomatoes in a bowl. Add the chicken and the sauce to the potatoes, then cover with foil and cook in the oven for a further 20 minutes until the chicken is cooked. Sprinkle over the freshly chopped oregano, if desired, and serve.

Tagliatelle with courgette flowers & chicken

This pasta dish is best served in the early summer when courgettes/zucchini are in season.

2 skinless, boneless chicken breasts
50 g/3 tablespoons unsalted butter
2 tablespoons olive oil
1 small onion, thinly sliced
200 g/2 cups small courgettes/zucchini,
    cut into thin julienne strips
1 garlic clove, crushed
2 teaspoons finely chopped fresh marjoram
350 g/12½ oz. dried tagliatelle
a large handful of courgette/zucchini flowers,
    thoroughly washed and stamens removed
sea salt and freshly ground black pepper
thinly shaved Parmesan cheese, to garnish

SERVES 4–6

Heat the grill/broiler to medium. Season the chicken and grill/broil for 25 minutes, turning once, until golden and cooked through. Cut into evenly sized pieces and put to one side.

Heat the butter and half the olive oil in a medium saucepan, add the onion and cook gently, stirring frequently, for about 5 minutes until softened. Add the courgettes to the pan and sprinkle over the garlic, marjoram and salt and pepper to taste.

Add the chicken pieces and cook for 8 minutes until the courgettes have coloured.

Set aside a few whole courgette flowers to garnish, then roughly shred the rest and add them to the pan. Stir to mix, taste and adjust the seasoning if required.

Meanwhile, cook the pasta in a pan of rolling boiling salted water until al dente. Drain the cooked pasta and tip it into the chicken mixture with the remaining oil. Serve topped with Parmesan cheese shavings and the reserved courgette flowers.

Crispy gravy spaghetti

Pan juices from a roast make one of the most flavourful sauces ever.

1.8 kg/4 lb. roasting chicken, skin
   patted dry with a paper towel/
   kitchen paper
3 onions, cut into wedges
3 sprigs of rosemary
3 sprigs of thyme
1 whole head garlic, top sliced off
extra virgin olive oil
250 ml/1 cup white wine
1 tablespoon tomato purée/paste,
1 chicken stock cube
1 tablespoon grated Parmesan cheese
500 g/1 lb. 2 oz. dried spaghetti
sea salt and freshly ground
   black pepper

a roasting pan just bigger than
   the chicken

SERVES 4–6

Preheat the oven to 200°C (400°F) Gas 6.

Place two onion wedges inside the cavity of the chicken along with a sprig of rosemary and thyme. Place the rest of the onion wedges in the bottom of the roasting pan.

Sit the chicken on top, add the garlic and massage a little olive oil into the chicken. Pour a glug of oil on the onions around the chicken. Season everything with salt and pepper.

Roast in the preheated oven for 10 minutes, then turn the heat down to 180°C (350°F) Gas 4. Pour the wine around the chicken (not onto it) and roast for a further 1 hour 20 minutes for a 1.8-kg/4-lb. chicken, or until the juices run clear.

In the last half hour of cooking, bring a large pan of salted water to a boil for the pasta.

Remove the cooked chicken from the roasting pan, place on a dish, cover in foil and leave to rest. Set the oven temperature to 220°C (420°F) Gas 7. Place the roasting pan over a low heat and deglaze. If necessary add another splash of wine, you should have about 1 cm/½ inch of gravy in the bottom of the pan.

Add the tomato purée and stock cube. As soon as the sauce looks rich and glossy, remove from the heat and stir in the cheese.

Cook the spaghetti in the salted boiling water for 4 minutes only (the usual cooking time is 12 minutes). Tip the hot drained pasta into the roasting pan and toss over a high heat until well coated in the gravy.

Spread evenly in the pan and return to the oven. Cook for 10 minutes at 220°C (420°F) Gas 7, then reduce the temperature to 200°C (400°F) Gas 6 for a further 10 minutes, or until bits of the pasta are crispy and the rest is al dente but not tough. Place the rested roast chicken on top of the crispy pasta. Pour over any juices and serve. If you like, you can take the pasta out 5 minutes early, place the chicken on top and return to the oven to crisp up the chicken skin before serving.

Chicken alfredo

Alfredo is the king of the fresh pasta sauces and a firm international favourite. It was invented in Rome, at a restaurant called Alfredo alla Scrofa (which, incidentally, means 'at the south'). This creamy delight was served by the restaurant owner, Alfredo, with a gold spoon and fork given to him by Douglas Fairbanks and Mary Pickford while on their honeymoon in 1927. Spinach (green) fettuccine is synonymous with Alfredo all over Italy, but this deliciously rich sauce makes anything it coats wonderful.

200 ml/generous ¾ cup double/heavy cream
125 g/1 stick butter
a pinch of freshly grated nutmeg
75 g/1 cup grated/shredded
Parmesan cheese (or half Parmesan and
   half pecorino cheese)
200 g/7 oz. cooked chicken pieces
200 g/7 oz. dried pasta or 170 g/6 oz.
   fresh pasta
sea salt and freshly ground black pepper

SERVES 2

Put a large pan of salted water on to boil for the pasta.

Meanwhile, to make the sauce, heat the cream, butter and nutmeg in a heavy-based pan over a medium heat for about 2–3 minutes, stirring occasionally, until the butter has melted into the cream.

Stir in the cheese and chicken, heat through and then remove from the heat. If the sauce is a little too runny, heat over a low heat until it is thickened. Season carefully – this dish rarely needs salt as the cheese imparts enough.

When the salted water is at a rolling boil, add the pasta and cook according to the packet instructions. Drain the pasta, but keep a cup of the cooking water. Tip the hot drained pasta into the sauce, adding a splash of the retained pasta cooking water. Toss over a high heat until the pasta looks well coated and creamy.

Serve immediately with plenty of extra freshly ground black pepper.

Mustard & herb chicken
baked in a salt crust

This chicken dish is so easy to prepare. You will be amazed at how beautifully succulent it is, as the salt crust keeps all the moisture in during cooking. As you are using egg whites to help bind the salt, save the yolks and make aïoli or mayonnaise (see page 59) to go with cold leftovers.

1.5–1.8-kg/3½–4 lb. chicken
1 lemon, cut in half
3 tablespoons Dijon mustard
1 tablespoon dried herbes de Provence
5 egg whites
1.8 kg/4 lb. coarse sea salt
freshly ground black pepper, to season

a roasting pan or baking dish similar in size to the chicken

SERVES 6

Preheat the oven to 190°C (375°F) Gas 5.

Stuff the chicken with the lemon halves and rub the mustard all over the skin. Sprinkle with the herbes de Provence and season with freshly ground black pepper. Set the chicken aside.

In a large bowl lightly beat the egg whites until frothy. Add the salt and mix thoroughly. The mixture should be the consistency of wet sand.

Spread a thin layer of salt evenly on the bottom of the roasting pan or baking dish. Put the chicken on top and cover with the rest of the salt mixture. Pat down well and make sure there are no holes through which the steam can escape.

Bake the chicken in the preheated oven for 1 hour. You'll notice that the salt will turn a golden brown. Remove the chicken from the oven and leave it to rest for 10 minutes.

Using the back of a knife, crack open the crust and remove. Put the chicken on a wooden board and carve. Serve immediately with accompaniments of your choice.

Garlic butter roast chicken

Roast chicken is an all-time favourite and always makes a great family meal. Adding the butter under the skin results in a moist, tasty chicken, aromatic from herbs and garlic. Serve with roasted or mashed potatoes, vegetables and any other trimmings of your choosing.

3 garlic cloves, 2 peeled and
  1 unpeeled
70 g/5 tablespoons butter, softened
2 tablespoons freshly chopped flat-leaf parsley
1 teaspoon fresh lemon thyme or thyme leaves
zest and fresh juice of ½ lemon, freshly grated
  & squeezed (save the lemon half after
  squeezing as it will be used in the recipe)
2-kg/4½-lb. roasting chicken
sea salt and ground black pepper

For the gravy
½ tablespoon olive oil
½ onion, finely chopped
1 fresh bay leaf
a splash of white wine
300 ml/1¼ cups chicken stock

SERVES 4

Preheat the oven to 200°C (400°F) Gas 6.

Make the garlic butter by pounding the peeled garlic into a paste with a pinch of salt. Mix together 50 g/ 3½ tablespoons of the butter with the garlic paste, parsley, lemon thyme and lemon zest.

Season the chicken with salt and pepper. Place on a rack in a roasting pan. Place the unpeeled garlic clove and the squeezed lemon half inside the chicken cavity. Pour over the lemon juice.

Using your fingers, gently pull the skin away from the chicken breast. Insert the garlic butter under the skin and on to the flesh, pressing down to spread it evenly over the chicken breast. Dot the remaining butter over the chicken legs and wings.

Roast the chicken in the preheated oven for 1 hour 20 minutes–1 hour 30 minutes, basting often with butter juices, until cooked through and the juices run clear. Rest for 15 minutes.

Meanwhile, use the roasting juices to make a gravy. Skim off excess fat from the roasting juices. Heat the oil in a pan, add the onion and bay leaf and fry gently until the onion has softened. Add the wine, cook briefly, then add the stock and the roasting juices. Bring to a boil and cook until slightly reduced. Season as required. Discard the bay leaf and serve at once with the chicken.

Chicken kievs

When buying chicken breasts for this, find the largest and plumpest possible; it will really help with keeping the garlic butter in the middle. If you're cutting up a whole chicken, remove the breast joints from the bone.

For the garlic butter

50 g/3½ tablespoons butter, softened
1 garlic clove, finely chopped
2 big pinches of fresh flat-leaf
    parsley, chopped
a fresh squeeze of lemon juice
    (approximately ¼ lemon;
    save the rest to serve)
sea salt and freshly ground
    black pepper

For the chicken

2 large skinless, boneless
    chicken breasts
1 teaspoon freshly chopped tarragon
40 g/5 tablespoons plain/
    all-purpose flour
3 eggs, beaten
100 g/2 cups dried breadcrumbs
300 ml/1¼ cups sunflower oil,
    for frying

To serve

salad leaves
potatoes, cooked as desired

SERVES 2

Start by mixing the garlic butter so you can chill it in the fridge to harden. Mix the butter, garlic, parsley and lemon juice in a bowl, and season with salt and pepper. Portion the butter into 2 flat, thin pieces, approximately 2.5 cm/1 inch wide and 5 cm/2 inches long, so that they'll slot into the cut in the chicken breast. Wrap in foil and put in the fridge to harden while you prepare the chicken.

Cut the 'false fillet' (the small piece of muscle on the side, which is attached, can be prised apart by pulling it) off the chicken breasts, as you're going to use this to plug the hole in the side. Lay each breast flat, push down on the top to level it and carefully slice through the middle, front to back, so that there's a cut down one side. Don't cut all the way through; the cut needs to go about three-quarters of the way through. Take the garlic butter from the fridge and place a piece inside each breast. Take the false fillet and push one end in first, at the edge of the cut, then slot the other end into the other end of the cut to help 'plug' it.

Mix the tarragon with the flour. Roll each stuffed breast in the seasoned flour, dip in the egg and then cover really well with breadcrumbs. Wrap in foil and place in the fridge for 30 minutes in order for them to 'set'.

Take the kievs out of the fridge and repeat the coating process: flour first, then egg and then breadcrumbs.

Heat the sunflower oil in a heavy-based pan or deep fryer until a cube of bread browns in 30 seconds. Carefully lower the kievs into the hot oil and fry for 20 minutes, or until cooked through, turning carefully once halfway through cooking.

Drain on paper towels/kitchen paper, then serve with a lemon quarter to squeeze over the top, salad leaves and potatoes.

Chicken with 40 cloves of garlic

Yes, this is truly a dish for garlic lovers! Pot-roasting the bird makes for tender, flavourful chicken, aromatic with tarragon. Serve the cooked whole garlic cloves with the chicken so that diners can squeeze the softened garlic out of the skins as a rich and tasty accompaniment.

1.8-kg/4-lb. roasting chicken
25 g/1½ tablespoons butter
1 tablespoon olive oil
40 garlic cloves, separated but unpeeled
100 ml/⅓ cup vermouth or dry white wine
juice of ½ lemon, freshly squeezed
200 ml/1 cup good-quality chicken stock
a handful of fresh tarragon sprigs
salt and freshly ground black pepper

a lidded flameproof casserole dish/Dutch Oven
  large enough to hold the chicken

SERVES 6

Preheat the oven to 180°C (350°F) Gas 4.

Season the chicken with salt and pepper. Heat the butter and olive oil in a large frying pan/skillet. Add the chicken and brown on all sides. Save the pan juices.

Meanwhile, heat the casserole dish/Dutch Oven on the stovetop. Transfer the browned chicken to the dish. Tuck some of the garlic cloves into the cavity, sprinkle the rest around the chicken and pour over the vermouth or wine. Allow to sizzle briefly, then pour in the buttery juices from the frying pan/skillet, the lemon juice and stock. Add the tarragon, placing a few sprigs of it inside the cavity of the chicken.

Bring to a boil on the stovetop, then cover with the lid and transfer the dish to the preheated oven. Bake, covered, for 1 hour 20 minutes–1 hour 30 minutes until the chicken is cooked through and the juices run clear.

Transfer the chicken to a serving dish. Use a slotted spoon to transfer the garlic cloves to the dish. Pour the juices into a serving jug/pitcher to use as a gravy, skimming off any excess fat. Serve the chicken with the garlic cloves and gravy.

Index

Credits

RECIPE CREDITS

Valerie-Aikman Smith
Indian pepper chicken
Mustard & herb chicken
baked in a salt crust
Sriracha & lime grilled
chicken wings
Cajun fried chicken

Miranda Ballard
Chicken Caesar sliders
Chicken kievs
Chicken tikka masala

Ghillie Basan
Lemon chicken kebabs
wrapped in aubergine
Spicy chicken kebabs
with ground almonds

Fiona Beckett
Coq au vin
Sautéed chicken with
white wine, pea &
tarragon sauce
Chicken with white wine
& chanterelles

Julz Beresford
Chicken with garlic

Maxine Clark
Chicken pot pie

Ross Dobson
Chicken shish kebabs
with garlic sauce

Ursula Ferrigno
Roast chicken with broad
beans & lemon
Tagliatelle with chicken &
courgette flowers

Carol Hilker
Buffalo bingo wings with
homemade ranch
dressing
Extra-crunchy crumbed
wings
Jerk chicken
Honey-fried chicken
Fried chicken & biscuit

sliders with sausage
gravy
"Chicks in a blanket" with
apple sauce & maple
syrup
Buttermilk-crumbed wings
Red hot buffalo wings
Damn hot wings
Spicy Thai-style fried
wings
Baked parmesan wings
Coconut curry wings

Jennifer Joyce
Chicken panini with
Gouda, red onion &
honey mustard dressing
Chicken panini with
Scamorza roasted
tomato & watercress

Jenny Linford
Chicken cacciatore
Yakitori-glazed
mushroom & chicken
skewers
Garlic butter roast chicken
Chicken with 40 cloves of
garlic

Loretta Liu
Chicken and potato
cream stew dumplings
Spicy chicken & shrimp
dumplings
Red curry chicken & lentil
bao

Uyen Luu
Vietnamese chicken salad
with hot mint

Dan May
Mango & chilli-marinated
chicken
Peruvian-style chilli &
garlic chicken with new
potatoes

Nitisha Patel
Smokin' fiery chicken
wings
Perfect chicken curry
Saffron Murgh Mughali

Louise Pickford
Creole spiced chicken
burger
Open chicken burger with
grilled vegetables
Chicken burger with herb
mayonnaise
Chicken steak burger with
Caesar dressing
Thai chicken burger with
mango, crispy shallots
& sweet chilli/chile
dressing
Deep-fried buttermilk
chicken burger with
'nduja & slaw

Laura Santini
Crispy gravy spaghetti
Chicken alfredo

Milli Taylor
Moroccan chicken puffs

Jenny Tschiesche
Spanish-style red pepper
& chicken bake
Cornflake chicken
nuggets with sweet
potato chips & roasted
cherry tomatoes
Chicken fajitas

Sunil Vijayakar
Butter chicken

Laura Washburn
Tandoori chicken grilled
cheese with mango
chutney & paneer naan
Chipotle chicken grilled
cheese with roasted
green peppers & queso
fresco
Chicken alfredo mac 'n'
cheese
Barbecue chicken & two
cheeses mac 'n' cheese
Barbecue chicken fries
Chicken mole burrito
Chipotle chicken tacos
Chicken & chorizo
quesadilla
Spanish-style chicken &
rice

PHOTOGRAPHY CREDITS

Ed Anderson Page 140

Jan Baldwin Pages 12, 81

Martin Brigdale Page 111

Peter Cassidy Pages 26,
32, 33, 35, 49, 88, 89, 203,
104, 121

Jonathan Gregson
Page 134

Louise Hagger Page 10

Richard Jung Pages 22, 25

Mowie Kay Pages 118, 122,
125

Erin Kunkel Pages 19, 87,
107

David Munns Pages 126,
128, 129

Steve Painter Pages 7, 31,
44, 46-49, 67, 68, 79, 91,
112, 114, 126, 139

Matt Russell Pages 94, 119,
127

Christopher Scholey
Pages 24, 130, 132

Toby Scott Pages 2, 29, 36,
38, 39, 43, 50, 55, 64, 74,
95, 96, 99

Ian Wallace Pages 57, 60,
135

Isobel Weild Pages 71, 73,
208

Kate Whitaker Pages 21,
80, 90

Clare Winfield Pages 3,
14-16, 28, 30, 52-54, 58, 70,
76, 83, 84, 97, 100, 101, 117,
137, 141